I0519464

The Invincible Blessings of Gratitude

Harris D. McFarlane

The Invincible Blessings of Gratitude

Copyright ©2023 Rev. Harris D. McFarlane

Paperback ISBN: 978-1-957809-64-9
eBook ISBN: 978-1-957809-65-6

All rights reserved. No part of this publication may be reproduced, distributed, or transmitted in any form or by any means, including photocopying, recording, or other electronic or mechanical methods without the prior written permission of the author except in the case of brief quotations embodied in reviews and certain other non-commercial uses permitted by copyright law. Otherwise stated Scripture quotations designated NIV are taken from the New International Version®.

Published by Cornerstone Publishing

A Division of Cornerstone Creativity Group LLC

Info@thecornerstonepublishers.com

www.thecornerstonepublishers.com

Author's Contact

To book the author to speak at your next event or to order bulk copies of this book, please, use the information below:

info@dimensionministries.org

Printed in the United States of America.

DEDICATION

To my wife, **Jennifer**, the woman who is both my dream come true and my best friend. Your support, insight, love, and encouragement have helped to make this book a reality. I love you!

To my daughter, **Nicole**, you have brought so much love, joy, purpose, and passion into my life. Being your dad is my greatest and most treasured reward. I Love you!

To everyone who reads and applies what you read in this book, may you enhance and create a happier and more joyful world.

CONTENTS

INTRODUCTION

In a world filled with chaos, disparity, and uncertainty, losing sight of the blessings surrounding us is easy. We are consumed by our needs, aspirations, and never-ending search for more. But what if there was a secret, a hidden key that could unlock a life of joy, contentment, and fulfillment? What if gratitude held the power to transform our existence?

Welcome to the world of "The Invincible Blessings of Gratitude," where we embark on a transformative journey that will revolutionize how you view the world and unlock the power of gratitude in your life. In this book, we will examine the foundational aspect of gratitude, understanding its essence and importance, particularly in the context of the Christian faith.

Gratitude, at its core, is more than just a fleeting feeling of appreciation. It is a mindset, a way of life, that allows us to recognize and embrace the blessings surrounding us. It is a powerful force that has the ability to shape our personalities, strengthen our spiritual connection with God, and have a significant impact on the world.

Throughout history, gratitude has been embedded in religious and spiritual teachings, and the Bible is no exception. It is rich with references to gratitude and its significance in our spiritual growth. From the Psalms of David, who poured out his heart in gratitude to the Lord, to the teachings of Jesus, who exemplified gratitude in even the most challenging times, we can find countless examples of the transformative power of gratitude.

This book will explore these biblical references of gratitude, delving into the stories and teachings that highlight its importance. We will uncover their wisdom and extract practical lessons that we can apply to our lives.

But this book is not just about theory; it is about practicality. We will also discuss the role of gratitude in cultivating stronger relationships, enhancing job satisfaction, and finding solace in times of abundance. We will provide you with a roadmap for applying gratitude in your daily life, offering various exercises and prompts for reflection that will help you cultivate a grateful mindset.

"The Invincible Blessings of Gratitude" is not just a book but an invitation. An invitation to embrace gratitude as a way of life and to experience the invincible blessings that await as you unlock the extraordinary power of gratitude. Whether you are a Christian seeking a deeper connection with God or someone searching for greater meaning and fulfillment, this book holds the key to transforming your life.

So, join us on this journey of discovery as we uncover the power of gratitude and learn how it can shape our lives and impact the world around us. Get ready to embark on a path of joy, contentment, and fulfillment like never before. The adventure begins now.

The Biblical Foundations of Gratitude

01

Gratitude, at its core, is a powerful force that can transform our lives. It is more than just a fleeting feeling of appreciation; it is a mindset, a way of life that allows us to recognize and embrace the blessings surrounding us. When we cultivate gratitude, we shift our focus from what we lack to what we have, from negativity to positivity. It is a perspective that brings joy, contentment, and fulfillment to our daily lives.

In a world driven by consumerism and constant striving for more, gratitude serves as a counterbalance. It reminds us to pause, reflect, and appreciate the abundance that already exists in our lives. It helps us overcome entitlement and materialism, fostering a sense of contentment and satisfaction.

Defining gratitude and its importance in the Christian faith

Gratitude is more than just a fleeting emotion or momentary expression of thanks. In the Christian landscape, gratitude is an altar—an intentional space to acknowledge and connect with God. Our faith, deeply interwoven with countless lessons, continually points towards the significance of gratitude, a spiritual discipline that echoes God's eternal love and benevolence.

Gratitude is an act! It is a positive emotion and a complex psychological state that involves recognizing and appreciating the kindness, help, generosity, and blessings received from someone or from life circumstances. It is a sincere feeling of thankfulness that arises when individuals acknowledge the good things they have or the positive actions of others that have benefited them.

In the Christian faith, gratitude goes beyond a mere expression of thanks. It is an attitude of the heart, recognizing God's goodness and faithfulness. It is a way of acknowledging His blessings and grace in our lives. It refers to the deep sense of thankfulness, appreciation, and acknowledgment of individuals towards God, fellow believers, and the blessings they have received. Gratitude is seen as a fundamental response to the grace and goodness of God, recognizing His provision, love, and mercy. It is not only about being thankful for material or tangible blessings but also about recognizing spiritual gifts, salvation, and the presence of God in one's life. It is often tied to humility. It is an act of understanding that everything we have, as Christians, comes from God's hand, and we do not deserve it purely on our own merit. *"A man can receive nothing, except it be given him from heaven"* (John 3:27).

The Bible emphasizes gratitude as a pivotal aspect of our

spiritual growth. In the Psalms, David repeatedly poured out his heart in gratitude to the Lord, even in the midst of trials and challenges. Jesus demonstrated gratitude when He gave thanks for the loaves and fish before feeding the multitude and when He expressed gratitude to God before raising Lazarus from the dead. Numerous biblical references aim to play a pivotal role in shaping the concept of gratitude in Christianity. One of the most renowned passages related to gratitude is found in the New Testament, in the book of Philippians 4:6-7:*"Be careful for nothing; but in every thing by prayer and supplication with thanksgiving let your requests be made known unto God. And the peace of God, which passeth all understanding, shall keep your hearts and minds through Christ Jesus."*

This passage highlights the idea that thanksgiving, or gratitude, is an essential element of communication with God. It encourages believers to bring their needs and desires to God while accompanied by a heart full of gratitude.

Furthermore, gratitude is often linked to worship in Christianity. It is expressed in prayers, songs, and acts of service. Believers are encouraged to give thanks in all circumstances, as stated in 1 Thessalonians 5:18:*"Give thanks in all circumstances; for this is the will of God in Christ Jesus for you."*

Gratitude is about being thankful for positive experiences

and trusting in God's sovereignty and wisdom, even in times of adversity or challenges. It, therefore, holds a central place in the Christian faith.

Gratitude is a way of honoring God, cultivating a deeper connection with Him, and acknowledging His sovereignty in our lives. It aligns our hearts with His will and opens the door to profoundly experiencing His love and blessings.

The Bible is filled with stories and teachings highlighting gratitude's transformative power. When we examine the apostle Paul's exhortations to give thanks in all circumstances, we see that gratitude is not just a fleeting emotion but a foundational principle for a life of faith.

Gratitude shapes our character and helps us develop humility, contentment, and compassion. It cultivates a heart of trust in God's providence and fosters a spirit of generosity and service towards others. It is the antidote to bitterness and ingratitude, allowing us to find solace in times of abundance and hope in times of adversity.

The Genesis of Gratitude: Recognizing Creation as the First Gift

God painted the universe with a masterful touch on the vast canvas of existence. The Book of Genesis chronicles this grand spectacle of creation. Every sunbeam, every gust of wind, the song of each bird, and the fragrance of every flower reflect His divine artistry.

Genesis 1:31:
"God saw all that He had made, and it was very good."

This verse is not just a statement; it is an invitation. Before our first steps or initial understanding of the world, God had already sown the seeds of gratitude. For every rhythmic heartbeat, every laughter line, and every tear shed, there is a deeper narrative of God's continuous act of creation. In addition, an authentic heart of thanksgiving emerges from this space of reflection.

In Genesis 1, the narrative describes the world's creation in a sequence of days. God creates the heavens, the earth, light, vegetation, animals, and finally, humankind. God looks upon His creation at the end of each day and pronounces it "good." However, the declaration changes on the sixth day, after creating humans. Genesis 1:31 encapsulates the completion of creation, emphasizing that not only was each individual component good but the entirety of creation was deemed "very good" by God Himself.

Here, the idea of gratitude emerges from the recognition that creation itself is a gift from God. With its intricate beauty, diverse life forms, and balanced ecosystems, the world is presented as a generous expression of God's creative power and love. This recognition sets the stage for gratitude because it prompts humans to acknowledge and appreciate the gift of existence and all it encompasses.

Tracing Gratitude through the Scriptures

The Bible is rich with moments where gratitude is a poignant backdrop. Gratitude is a pervasive and recurring theme throughout the Bible, spanning both the Old and New Testaments. It is a fundamental attitude of the heart that believers are encouraged to cultivate in their relationship with God and one another. From the very beginning of creation to the culmination of God's redemptive plan, gratitude is depicted as an essential response to God's goodness, grace, and provision.

The Bible opens with the creation story, where God brings the world into existence and declares it "good." This act of creation sets the stage for gratitude, as humans are called to recognize the beauty and harmony of the world and give thanks to the Creator for His wondrous works.

The Israelites, freshly delivered from Egyptian bondage, sang a song of thanksgiving by the Red Sea's shores.

The Book of Psalms is rich with expressions of gratitude and praise. Many psalms are dedicated to thanking God for His steadfast love, faithfulness, and deliverance. King David danced before the Lord with all his might, expressing profound gratitude for the Ark's return.

Psalm 136:1:
"Give thanks to the Lord, for he is good. His love endures forever."

Fast forward to the New Testament, and gratitude takes on an even deeper hue. In the New Testament, gratitude takes on new dimensions through the teachings and life of Jesus Christ. His parables often highlight the importance of recognizing God's gifts and using them responsibly. The story of the ten lepers (Luke 17:11-19) underscores the significance of giving thanks and returning to praise God for His healing.

The Last Supper, a cornerstone of Christian remembrance, is interlaced with thanksgiving. As Jesus broke bread, symbolizing His body given for many, gratitude intertwined with sacrifice, pointing to humanity's salvation. *"And when he had given thanks, he broke it and said, 'This is my body, which is for you; do this in remembrance of me"* (1 Corinthians 11:24).

The apostle Paul's letters emphasize gratitude as a transformative attitude. He encourages believers to *"Give thanks in all circumstances; for this is the will of God in Christ Jesus for you"* (1 Thessalonians 5:18). Paul links gratitude with God's will and the experience of His peace.

The New Testament chronicles are not just theological treatizes but encapsulate the lived experiences of early Christian communities. They faced tumultuous times, persecution, and societal ostracization. Yet their letters and narratives pulsate with gratitude.

Philippians 4:6:
"Do not be anxious about anything, but in every situation, by prayer and petition, with thanksgiving, present your requests to God."

This profound understanding illuminates the soul of early Christianity. Gratitude, for them, wasn't just reactive; it was proactive, shaping their worldview, acting as the antidote to challenges, and serving as the cornerstone for community building.

Gratitude and God's Will

The Bible, serving as a spiritual compass for believers, frequently emphasizes the importance of gratitude. One of its pivotal appeals is in 1 Thessalonians 5:18: *"Give thanks in all circumstances; for this is God's will for you in Christ Jesus."* This scripture is more than a mere suggestion; it presents a divine mandate. But the profundity of this verse lies in its scope—"all circumstances."

Gratitude, as articulated in this scripture, is not restricted to moments of prosperity, joy, or ease. It is an unwavering attitude that persists through adversities, heartaches, and uncertainties. Such encompassing gratitude aligns believers with the very will of God, transforming every sigh of thankfulness into an act of worship. This underscores the idea that gratitude should not be contingent on favorable circumstances but should be a consistent attitude, regardless of external factors.

Paul asserts that such a disposition of gratitude aligns with God's will for believers. In other words, cultivating gratitude is a virtue and a direct expression of living in harmony with God's desires for His people. This verse highlights that gratitude is a transformative attitude that reflects a deep understanding of God's grace, draws believers closer to Christ, and shapes their identity as His followers.

Gratitude in the Life of Jesus

The life of Jesus Christ is a beacon for Christians across epochs, illuminating a path of love, sacrifice, and compassion. Many revere Him for His miracles, teachings, and the unparalleled sacrifice He made for humanity. However, among these monumental acts and profound teachings lies a subtler yet equally powerful theme: gratitude. His life was not just a testament to God's power and love but also to a heart brimming with thankfulness.

Analysis of Jesus' gratitude-filled moments:

1. Feeding of the 5,000:

Imagine a sprawling crowd, their hearts hungry for spiritual sustenance and their bodies longing for physical nourishment. Among this multitude, only five loaves of bread and two fish were available. The stage was set for a miracle, but before anything else, Jesus showcased an essential virtue.

Matthew 14:19 narrates, "Taking the five loaves and the two fish and looking up to heaven, he gave thanks and broke the loaves." Before the miraculous multiplication, before satisfying the hunger of thousands, Jesus paused to express gratitude for the little He had. In this act, He demonstrated that gratitude isn't about abundance; it's a heart posture.

2. The Last Supper:

As dusk settled on that fateful evening, Jesus sat with His disciples, fully conscious of the sacrifice He was soon to make. Amidst this somber ambiance, where the weight of the impending crucifixion loomed heavy, gratitude once again shone brightly.

Luke 22:19 recounts, "And he took bread, gave thanks and broke it, and gave it to them, saying, 'This is my body given for you; do this in remembrance of me.'" Even as shadows of betrayal and sacrifice crept closer, Jesus's heart remained anchored in thankfulness, emphasizing the significance of gratitude even in the face of adversity.

3. Jesus healing the ten lepers and the gratefulness of one:

Among the many healed by Jesus, the story of the ten lepers stands out, not just for the healing but for the profound lesson on gratitude that followed. While all ten received their miracles, only one turned back, his heart overflowing with gratitude.

Luke 17:15-17 captures this poignant moment: "One of them, when he saw he was healed, came back, praising God in a loud voice. He threw himself at Jesus' feet and thanked him—and he was a Samaritan. Jesus asked, 'Were not all ten cleansed? Where are the other nine?'" This narrative is more than just a recounting of an event; it's a clarion call, urging believers to be the one who remembers to return, to recognize, and to express heartfelt thanks.

Emulating Jesus' heart of thanks.

Gratitude, as exemplified by Jesus, is more than just a fleeting emotion. It's a way of life—an intentional choice to recognize and appreciate the blessings, be they monumental or minute. The acts of Jesus beckon us not to admire them from a distance but to incorporate them into the fabric of our lives.

At various points in our lives, we have played the role of the ten lepers—recipients of blessings, grace, and miracles. The challenge, however, lies in choosing to be the one who returns and doesn't let life's hustle or challenges overshadow the countless reasons to be grateful. Let the life of Jesus inspire and challenge us. In every moment, amidst trials and triumphs, may we always find a reason to give thanks, emulating the heart of our Savior.

Start Implementing Gratitude Now

Gratitude, when fostered daily, becomes more than a sporadic response; it evolves into a life-altering perspective. For those desiring to solidify this foundation in their lives:

- *Start a gratitude journal:* Take a few minutes each day to write down three things you are grateful for. Reflect on the blessings, big or small, that you have experienced.

- *Practice gratitude in prayer:* Incorporate gratitude into your daily prayers. Begin by expressing thanks to God for specific things or people in your life.

- *Share your gratitude with others:* Take the time to express your gratitude to those around you. Write a note, send a message, or simply say "thank you" to someone who has positively impacted your life.

- *Cultivate a mindful presence:* Be present in the moment and cultivate awareness of the blessings around you. Notice the beauty in nature, the kindness of others, and the simple joys of life.

- *Choose a gratitude mantra:* Create a phrase or affirmation that reminds you to be grateful throughout the day. Repeat it whenever you find yourself slipping into negativity or discontentment.

We can unlock its extraordinary power by implementing these practical tips and embracing gratitude as a way of life. Gratitude strengthens our relationships, enhances our job satisfaction, and deepens our spiritual connection with God. As we cultivate a grateful mindset, we experience personal transformation, and on the other hand, we inspire and encourage others to embrace this life-changing perspective.

Embarking on the journey of gratitude is more than a fleeting endeavor; it is an intentional commitment to viewing life through God's enduring love and faithfulness. As we build this foundation, we find ourselves more attuned to God's whispers, more appreciative of His works, and more aligned with His will.

CHAPTER'S REFLECTION

- Gratitude goes beyond a simple feeling of thankfulness; it is a spiritual posture that encompasses acknowledging God's goodness, grace, and provision in all aspects of life. It involves expressing thanks, not just for material blessings but for the gift of salvation and the ongoing relationship with God.

- Gratitude is intertwined with worship, humility, and trust in God's plan, serving as a foundation for a deeper connection with God and fellow believers.

- Gratitude is not merely a concept found in isolated verses but woven into the fabric of the entire biblical narrative. It is a recurring call for believers to recognize God's blessings, respond with thankful hearts, and live in constant awareness of His goodness. From the first pages of Genesis to the final chapters of Revelation, gratitude remains an enduring theme that reflects the believer's relationship with the Creator and their fellow human beings.

Benefits of Gratitude

02

The sun has risen countless times, painting the sky with hues of orange, pink, and gold. Yet, each sunrise remains a miracle, a symbol of hope, renewal, and gratitude. As we journey through life, we often overlook the blessings sprinkled throughout our days. In this chapter, we explore the profound benefits of gratitude, diving deep into its physical, emotional, relational, and spiritual dimensions.

Practicing gratitude holds numerous benefits for Christians, extending beyond mere positivity to enriching their spiritual lives and overall well-being.

A Deeper Dive into Gratitude's Blessings

Throughout human history, across cultures and religions, gratitude has been heralded as a virtue. While many acknowledge its emotional or spiritual value, few recognize gratitude's profound physical and relational impacts. Gratitude is not just a fleeting feeling but a transformative force influencing our bodies, minds, and interactions.

1. **Physical Benefits:** The Health Implications of Being Thankful

   a. *The Science Behind Gratitude and Health:* Modern research increasingly highlights the tangible health benefits of gratitude. The practice of gratitude has been extensively studied within the realm of psychology and the health sciences, revealing a range of physical, emotional, and mental health benefits. Those who regularly practice gratitude have been found to enjoy better sleep, experience reduced pain levels, and even have a bolstered immune system. We might add more healthy years to our lives by counting our blessings.

   b. *Gratitude's Role in Stress Reduction:* Stress is inevitable in today's fast-paced world. However, here is a remedy that does not come in a bottle: gratitude. Grateful individuals tend to exhibit lower levels of perceived stress. Gratitude helps shift focus away from stressors and negative aspects of life, contributing to better stress management. By shifting our focus from what we lack to what we have, gratitude reduces cortisol levels, our body's primary stress hormone. This does not just mean a happier disposition but also a healthier heart and a sharper mind.

   c. *Overall Well-being and Quality of Life:* People who integrate gratitude into their daily routine often report increased vitality and energy. Gratitude is linked to increased levels of positive emotions such as joy, happiness, and contentment. It promotes a sense of overall well-being and life satisfaction. This zest for life is not merely about the absence of illness but a holistic sense of well-being and a deeper satisfaction with life as it unfolds.

2. **Emotional Benefits:** Gratitude's Impact on Joy, Happiness, and Overall Mood

   a. The Neurological Aspects of Gratitude: The brain loves gratitude. Every time we immerse ourselves in feelings of thankfulness, our brain releases dopamine and serotonin, the "feel-good" neurotransmitters. Numerous studies have shown that practicing gratitude is associated with reduced symptoms of depression, anxiety, and stress. Grateful individuals tend to have a more positive outlook on life and are better equipped to cope with challenging situations. Over time, by consistently practicing gratitude, we can rewire our brains to feel happier and more positive.

   b. Balancing Negative Emotions: Life has its valleys alongside its peaks. In times of heartache or anxiety, gratitude serves as an anchor. By drawing attention to the silver linings, even during storms, gratitude acts as a buffer against depression and pervasive negativity.

   Proverbs 15:13:
   "A happy heart makes the face cheerful, but heartache crushes the spirit."

This ancient wisdom captures the essence of gratitude's emotional benefits. A heart infused with gratitude radiates happiness, and this joy undeniably becomes our strength.

3. **Relational Benefits:** How Gratitude Can Improve Our Relationships with Others and with God

   a. *Expressing Gratitude in Interpersonal Relationships:* A simple "thank you" can work wonders. We strengthen bonds, build trust, and foster mutual respect by expressing our appreciation. Relationships thrive when acknowledgment and appreciation flow freely.

   b. *Gratitude's Role in Conflict Resolution:* Conflicts are inevitable, but their resolution becomes smoother in an environment of gratitude. Thankfulness allows us to see the other person's perspective, reduces defensive postures, and paves the way for reconciliation.

   c. *Deepening our Relationship with God:* Every whispered "thank you" directed heavenward deepens our intimacy with God. We acknowledge God's ceaseless blessings through gratitude, drawing closer to His benevolent heart with each expression of thanks.

"Therefore encourage one another and build each other up, just as in fact, you are doing." (*1* Thessalonians 5:11). Gratitude, in its

essence, is an act of encouragement. By showing appreciation, we uplift the spirits of those around us, strengthening the ties that bind us to one another and to God.

4.   **Spiritual Benefits:** How Gratitude Can Lead to a Deeper Connection with God

a.   Gratitude as a Form of Worship: Each time we bow our heads in thanks, we participate in an ancient form of worship. Recognizing God as the fountain of all blessings, we offer our deepest thanks, aligning ourselves with His will and purpose. Gratitude fuels heartfelt worship. When believers express thanksgiving for God's goodness, it naturally leads to worship and praise, creating a more meaningful and authentic worship experience.

b.   The Role of Gratitude in Spiritual Growth: Gratitude accelerates spiritual maturity. A thankful heart is a fertile ground for divine truths to take root, grow, and flourish. As we express our thanks for life's blessings, big or small, we progress on our spiritual path, gaining wisdom and insight. Incorporating gratitude into prayers deepens communication with God. Gratitude-filled prayers balance requests with expressions of thanks, leading to a more intimate prayer life.

c.   The Transformative Power of a Thankful Heart: The Bible is replete with narratives of individuals transformed by gratitude. From lepers healed and then returning to offer thanks to

David's psalms of gratitude, these stories serve as testaments to the transformative power of a thankful heart.

Understanding How Gratitude Improves Mental Health

Gratitude has been shown to significantly impact mental health by fostering positive emotions, promoting resilience, and improving overall psychological well-being. Gratitude can transform our mental health and emotional well-being. We can develop resilience, combat negative emotions, and cultivate a sense of purpose and meaning by cultivating gratitude.

1. Cultivating Resilience

Life is filled with challenges and setbacks, but gratitude can help us navigate them resiliently. By focusing on what we are grateful for, even in difficult times, we can reframe our perspective and find the strength to persevere. Gratitude allows us to find silver linings, learn from adversity, and grow from our experiences. It enhances psychological resilience, which is the ability to bounce back from adversity. When individuals regularly acknowledge their blessings, they develop a reservoir of positive emotions and experiences that can serve as coping mechanisms during tough times.

2. Combating Negative Emotions

Gratitude is a powerful antidote to negative emotions such as stress, anxiety, and depression. By shifting our attention to the things we are grateful for, we can interrupt negative thought patterns and replace them with positive ones, leading to a decrease in feelings of anxiety and sadness. This shift in focus helps us cultivate a more optimistic outlook on life and improves our overall mental well-being. Engaging in gratitude exercises or simply reflecting on things to be thankful for can elevate the mood and counteract negative emotions.

3. Finding Purpose and Meaning

Practicing gratitude opens our eyes to the abundance and beauty that surround us. It helps us recognize the small moments of joy and appreciate the interconnectedness of all things. We can find purpose and meaning in our lives by fostering a grateful mindset, leading to greater fulfillment and satisfaction. Many people are living below their God-given potential. They live powerless lives of love, joy, peace, harmony, and satisfaction. They don't know how to harness and cultivate the most magnificent power within themselves. This power of gratitude can awaken inside us and transform our destiny. Two psychologists, Dr. Robert A. Emmons of the University of California and Dr. Michael E. McCullough of the University of Miami, have done extensive research on the power of gratitude. In one of their studies, they asked associates to write a few sentences each week, concentrating on the appropriate subjects. One group wrote about things they were grateful for that had developed during the week. The second group wrote about everyday circumstances that were irritable or things that were unpleasant to them. The third group wrote about things that had impacted them, with no necessary focus on negative or positive things. About ten weeks later, those who wrote about gratitude were much more buoyant and cheerful and felt better about their future. Amazingly, they also engaged in much more physical exercise and had fewer visits to the doctor's office than those who were more stressed and aggravated. So, Dr. Robert Emmons, the world's leading scientific expert on gratitude, reveals why gratitude is good for our bodies, our minds, and our relationships. In a study of more than one thousand people from ages eight to eighty, he found that people who practice gratitude consistently report a magnitude of benefits, including improved physical and psychological health, stronger relationships, increased resilience, and greater happiness and life satisfaction. He emphasized that gratitude is a skill that can be developed through consistent practice, and its effects can be life-changing. By intentionally cultivating gratitude, we can unlock its extraordinary power and experience its profound impact on our lives.

I have personally experienced the transformative impact this practice can have on my life. I made a conscious decision to embrace gratitude as a way of life.

I started a gratitude journal where I would write down three to seven things that I was grateful for every day. Initially, it felt unnatural. However, as I persisted, I noticed a subtle shift in my perspective. For example, I thank God that he woke me up each day; I thank Him for my health, my family's health, the sunrise, fresh air, freedom, and a personal relationship with Him. These first few minutes always set the direction for my day.

With time, gratitude became a habit, and its impact on my life has been profound. I became more resilient in the face of challenges as I focused on the positive aspects of each situation. I became more present and appreciative of the moments that brought me joy. Moreover, expressing gratitude in my relationships deepened my connections, fostering love, understanding, forgiveness, and more peace of mind. The Bible has over 400 verses that talk about gratitude and thanksgiving.

The Holistic Blessings of Gratitude

Gratitude is a central and significant concept that holds holistic blessings for individuals and communities alike. Gratitude is more than just a simple expression of thankfulness; it encompasses a deep sense of appreciation and recognition of God's goodness and blessings. Gratitude is not just a single note; it is a symphony. Its melodies resonate in our bodies, minds, relationships, and spiritual journeys. The benefits of gratitude are manifold and interwoven into every facet of our existence.

By recognizing the apparent and concealed blessings, we nurture a state of well-being that transcends fleeting pleasures or transient sorrows. A grateful heart shines as a beacon of hope and resilience in a world often marked by cynicism, uncertainty, and strife.

Embracing gratitude, we find a bridge between the earthly and the divine, the mundane and the profound. It strengthens the relationship between believers and God. Through gratitude, we would discover that God is not just in the miracles but also in the mundane, seeing His hand in every smile, every kind gesture, every sunset, and every new dawn. When individuals recognize and appreciate God, they are drawn into a more intimate relationship with Him.

Incorporating gratitude into our daily rituals doesn't merely add years to our lives; it adds life to our years. It's not just about uttering words of thanks but about cultivating an attitude that sees and appreciates the silver linings even in the stormiest clouds.

As we close this chapter, let's make a conscious commitment. Let's pledge not to let gratitude be an occasional guest but a permanent resident in our hearts. In recognizing and celebrating our blessings, we don't just enrich our lives; we shine a light, illuminating the path for others and guiding them toward a life of contentment, purpose, and divine connection.

Remember, a grateful heart is a magnet for miracles. By understanding and cherishing the holistic benefits of gratitude, we set ourselves on a path to a more fulfilling, enriched, and joyous life, drawing closer to others, ourselves, and, most importantly, God.

The Danger of Ingratitude

Ingratitude, a seemingly innocuous emotion, poses profound spiritual and psychological dangers. Rooted in a lack of thankfulness, this sentiment can potentially detach us from the essence of God's love and blessings. The danger of ingratitude is often highlighted to encourage believers to cultivate a thankful and appreciative attitude. The Holy Bible serves as an instrument to navigate these emotional complexities, shedding light on the pitfalls of ingratitude and pointing us toward a life imbued with thanksgiving. The Bible provides several teachings that underscore gratitude's importance and warn against ingratitude's negative consequences. Here are a few key points:

1. *Spiritual Stagnation:* Gratitude is often seen as a catalyst for spiritual growth and maturity. Recognizing and appreciating God's grace and blessings encourages believers to grow in faith, trust, and devotion. Conversely, ingratitude can lead to spiritual stagnation as it inhibits the development of a deeper relationship with God. A classic example of ingratitude leading to spiritual decline can be found in Romans 1:21. Here, the scripture aptly states, *"For although they knew God, they did not honor him as God or give thanks to him, but they became futile in their thinking, and their foolish hearts were darkened."* This

makes it clear that when gratitude is absent, our spiritual understanding of God can be clouded, leading us to spiritual decay.

2. *Barriers to Relationship with God:* The Bible teaches that God is the source of all blessings, and when we fail to acknowledge and thank Him for these blessings, we risk distancing ourselves from His presence. It is also akin to turning our backs on a loved one who constantly showers us with gifts. Just as not acknowledging a friend's kindness can strain the friendship, not recognizing God's blessings can create a rift in our spiritual connection with Him. Ingratitude can lead to a spiritual disconnect from God.

3. *Increased Vulnerability to Temptation:* The scripture in Deuteronomy 8:12-14 warns about the dangers of forgetting the Lord and His blessings. When one starts to believe, "My power and the might of my hand have gotten me this wealth," it's a clear sign of pride. This misplaced self-belief and arrogance can easily steer one towards sinful temptations.

4. *Psychological Implications:* On a psychological level, ingratitude is like a poison. Ingratitude can foster a spirit of discontent and unhappiness. It breeds negative emotions, and these emotions can spiral into darker thoughts. A person who constantly compares their life to others and fails to acknowledge their blessings may be consumed with envy. When people focus on what they lack rather than what they have been given, they

tend to feel unsatisfied and constantly yearn for more. This can lead to a cycle of seeking fulfillment in material possessions or worldly achievements rather than finding contentment in God's provision. Over time, this can manifest as anxiety, depression, and dissatisfaction with life.

5. *Entitlement and Materialistic Mindsets:* Entitlement and materialism are pervasive mindsets in our society that can hinder our ability to experience gratitude. These mindsets stem from a belief that we deserve more and that our worth is determined by what we possess. However, they can lead to dissatisfaction, greed, and a constant desire for more, preventing us from truly appreciating what we already have.

6. *Lack of Generosity and Compassion:* Gratitude often leads to a compassionate and giving heart. When individuals are grateful for their blessings, they are more likely to extend kindness and generosity to others. Ingratitude, however, can lead to a self-centered attitude that hinders the willingness to share one's blessings with those in need.

Overall, the danger of ingratitude in Christianity lies in its potential to disrupt individuals' spiritual, emotional, and relational well-being. Cultivating gratitude is considered essential for a healthy Christian life, as it reflects an acknowledgment of God's sovereignty, goodness, and provision while guarding against the negative consequences of an ungrateful heart.

Throughout the Bible, numerous teachings warn against the dangers of materialism and the pursuit of wealth. One such example is the story of the rich young ruler who was unwilling to give up his possessions to follow Jesus. This story is a powerful reminder that our attachment to material possessions can hinder our spiritual growth and prevent us from experiencing the true blessings of gratitude.

CHAPTER'S REFLECTION

- Practicing gratitude holds numerous benefits for Christians, extending beyond mere positivity to enriching their spiritual lives and overall well-being.

- Gratitude helps individuals maintain a humble and receptive heart, recognizing God's hand in their lives and fostering a deeper appreciation for His blessings. It's a way of acknowledging God's love, grace, and provision, and it's considered an antidote to the spiritual dangers posed by ingratitude.

- Gratitude is often regarded as a significant virtue, and ingratitude is seen as a spiritual danger.

Gratitude
in Adversity
and Trials

03

In the face of adversity and trials, gratitude is a significant aspect of Christian faith and practice. While expressing gratitude during difficult times may seem counterintuitive, the Bible and Christian teachings emphasize the importance of nurturing a thankful heart even in challenging circumstances.

Life is an unpredictable journey filled with both triumphs and setbacks. Adversity and trials are inevitable companions along our path, testing our resilience and pushing us to our limits. However, amidst the hardships and struggles, there is a powerful tool that can help us navigate these challenging times with grace and strength: gratitude. Cultivating gratitude can give us a fresh perspective, allowing us to find silver linings and valuable lessons even in the darkest moments of our lives.

Gratitude in adversity and trials is a fundamental aspect of the Christian faith that underscores the importance of maintaining a thankful heart even when faced with challenges. Amid difficulties, we are called to express gratitude as a way to demonstrate trust in

God's faithfulness, shift our perspective, and cultivate spiritual growth. This perspective acknowledges that adversity offers opportunities for character refinement, and by choosing gratitude, believers exemplify their unwavering trust in God's plan and His ability to bring blessings even amidst hardship.

When we actively practice gratitude, we shift our focus from what is lacking to what we already possess. It allows us to acknowledge the blessings that exist even in the midst of adversity, no matter how small. This change in perspective can be transformative, empowering us to withstand the trials that come our way.

Finding Light in the Darkness

Feeling overwhelmed, discouraged, and even defeated during adversity is natural. However, cultivating gratitude can help us find light in the darkness. By intentionally seeking out the positive aspects of our situation, we can uncover hidden opportunities, moments of growth, and sources of strength that might have otherwise gone unnoticed. Gratitude reminds us that, despite adversity, there is always something to be grateful for.

Gratitude is a powerful tool for building resilience in the face of adversity. When we focus on the positive aspects of our lives, we develop an inner strength that helps us weather the storms that come our way. Gratitude fosters a sense of hope and optimism, enabling us to face challenges with courage and determination. By acknowledging and appreciating the support, love, and kindness of others during tough times, we create a network of support that can carry us through even the most difficult trials.

During life's challenges, storms, and unexpected tragedies, the idea of feeling gratitude might seem strange and even out of place. However, from a Christian perspective, adversity does not negate the essence of gratitude; it can often amplify it. When one delves into the teachings and stories of the Bible, a profound message emerges about the depth of gratitude one can find even in the harshest of life's circumstances.

Christian Perspective

The Book of James offers a perspective on hardship that is transformative.

James 1:2-4
"My brethren, count it all joy when ye fall into divers temptations; Knowing this, that the trying of your faith worketh patience. But let patience have her perfect work, that ye may be perfect and entire, wanting nothing."

It does not merely instruct believers to tolerate or endure adversities but to embrace them with a spirit of joy. This joy does not stem from the trial itself but from understanding the refining process it instigates. Through trials, one's faith is tested, fostering perseverance, which matures the believer and makes them complete in their faith.

Adversity and trials present us with valuable opportunities for personal growth and self-reflection. When we approach these challenges with gratitude, we open ourselves up to the possibility of learning profound lessons. Difficult times often reveal our inner strength, resilience, and capacity for adaptation. We can transform our trials into stepping stones toward a stronger and wiser self by expressing gratitude for the lessons learned and the personal growth achieved.

Turning to the life of Jesus Christ provides a beautiful and poignant example of this principle in action. On the eve of His crucifixion, aware of the imminent suffering, Jesus expressed gratitude. The Last Supper, a significant event for Christians, showcases Jesus breaking bread and giving thanks. This act, steeped in the symbolism of sacrifice, reveals the profound nature of gratitude in the face of adversity.

Paul's letter to the Romans gives further insight into the purpose of adversity.

Romans 5:3-5

"Not only that, but we rejoice in our sufferings, knowing that suffering produces endurance, and endurance produces

character, and character produces hope, and hope does not put us to shame, because God's love has been poured into our hearts through the Holy Spirit who has been given to us."

Suffering, though painful, is not meaningless. It cultivates perseverance, which refines one's character, and from that refined character springs hope. This hope is anchored in the unwavering love of God, which believers experience through the Holy Spirit.

A vital element underpinning this perspective is faith. In the New Testament, *"Faith is described as having assurance and confidence in the unseen"* (Hebrews 11:1). So, even when surrounded by adversity with no clear end in sight, a Christian's faith enables them to trust in God's larger, benevolent plan.

Also, in the Psalm, we encounter the raw emotions of David, a man who faced various adversities. Yet, even when beset by enemies, in deep despair, or facing personal failures, David often turned to God in praise and gratitude. His psalms serve as a testament to the power of gratitude as a bulwark against despair and a conduit for connection with the all-powerful God.

Psalm 31:7
"I will be glad and rejoice in Your mercy, For You have considered my trouble; You have known my soul in adversities."

However, not just personal strength and individual faith foster gratitude. The Christian community plays an instrumental role in this journey. The early Christian communities, as seen in the letters of Paul, were places of mutual encouragement. When one member faltered or faced overwhelming challenges, the community stepped in, reminding them of God's faithfulness and the hope they shared.

Essentially, the Christian perspective on gratitude in adversity isn't about ignoring pain or hardship. It's about viewing these challenges through a different lens—a lens of faith, hope, and divine purpose. It's about recognizing that even in the darkest moments, there's an ever-present opportunity to connect more deeply with God, to grow in faith, and to discover a richer, more profound sense of gratitude.

Take, for instance, the story of Joseph. Sold into slavery by his own brothers, falsely accused, and imprisoned, he faced one adversity after another. However, Joseph's story is not merely a chronicle of misfortunes; it is a testament to the providence of God. Years later, when confronting his brothers, he professed, "*You intended to harm me, but God intended it for good*" (Genesis 50:20). This profound acknowledgment embodies the essence of seeing divine purpose even in hardship. Joseph's gratitude wasn't for the suffering itself but for the greater narrative of redemption and purpose that God was weaving through his life.

Another figure, Job, encountered unprecedented adversity, quickly losing his wealth, health, and children. Yet, amidst his lamentations and desperate search for answers, Job exclaimed, *"Though he slay me, yet will I hope in him"* (Job 13:15). This unwavering trust is a testament to the depth of Job's faith and his profound gratitude for the relationship he had with the Almighty, even when he was at the nadir of his suffering.

In the New Testament, the Apostle Paul, no stranger to suffering himself, shared a profound insight: *"For our light and momentary troubles are achieving for us an eternal glory that far outweighs them all"* (2 Corinthians 4:17). Paul, beaten, imprisoned, and persecuted, found a deeper truth in his adversities. They were momentary in the light of eternity, shaping him (and his readers) for a divine and glorious purpose. His writings radiate gratitude, not because he enjoyed suffering but because he had an eternal perspective.

The early Christian church, too, was rife with persecution. Yet the spirit of gratitude was palpable. In Acts, after Peter and John were released from a harsh interrogation, the believers didn't respond with fear or lament; instead, they prayed and praised God. Their gratitude was rooted not in the absence of adversity but in the presence of God amidst their challenges.

The recurring theme is evident: adversity, from a Christian perspective, is not an endpoint but a journey, a refining process. Gratitude is not always about the immediate circumstances but about the bigger picture. This gratitude is nurtured by a deep-seated belief in God's sovereignty, awareness of His unchanging love, and the hope of available redemption. Through the annals of biblical history, we are reminded that even in the crucible of adversity, when approached with faith, there is always room for a heart brimming with gratitude.

Trials are life's inevitabilities. Yet nestled within them are unparalleled opportunities to discern God's relentless faithfulness. As we journey through life's varied terrains, let gratitude be our compass, guiding us, strengthening us, and revealing God's omnipresence in every challenge.

In the crucible of hardships, gratitude's emergence might appear mysterious. Yet, it serves as a transformative tool. It anchors our faith when doubts threaten to capsize us. Instead of drowning in the magnitude of our problems, gratitude shifts our gaze toward God's enduring presence, providing a lifeline of hope. This perspective doesn't trivialize pain but empowers us to confront it with resilience and courage. A grateful heart recognizes trials not as arbitrary cruelties but as pathways, albeit rugged, to spiritual growth and deeper communion with God.

Contemporary Examples

Here are a few examples of individuals who have demonstrated gratitude in the face of trials:

1. *Nelson Mandela:* Nelson Mandela's life and leadership are indeed characterized by his ability to display gratitude and resilience in the face of immense trials and adversity. Mandela

was a South African anti-apartheid revolutionary who became the country's first black president after spending 27 years in prison for his involvement in the struggle against apartheid, a system of racial segregation and discrimination. Despite enduring 27 years of imprisonment during the apartheid era in South Africa, Nelson Mandela emerged with a spirit of forgiveness and gratitude. He expressed gratitude for the lessons he learned and the strength he gained during his confinement. Mandela's ability to find gratitude even in the most adverse circumstances played a crucial role in his leadership and the peaceful transition of South Africa into a democratic nation.

2. *Malala Yousafzai:* Malala is a Pakistani female education activist and Nobel laureate who has demonstrated tremendous gratitude and resilience in the face of severe trials and adversity. She faced a life-threatening ordeal when the Taliban shot her for advocating for girls' rights to education. Her remarkable story is an inspiring example of how one can maintain a positive attitude and a commitment to their cause even in the most challenging circumstances. Following the attack on her, Malala received an outpouring of support and solidarity from people worldwide. She expressed deep gratitude for the prayers, well wishes, and assistance she received during her recovery. She channeled her gratitude into an unwavering commitment to continue her activism, becoming an international symbol of

resilience and hope. Malala has used her platform to advocate for the education of girls globally, acknowledging the importance of international support in advancing her cause.

3. *Nick Vujicic:* Nick Vujicic is a motivational speaker and author born with a rare condition called tetra-amelia syndrome, which left him without limbs. Despite the immense challenges he faced due to his physical condition, Nick has demonstrated remarkable gratitude and resilience in the face of trials throughout his life. Born without arms and legs, Nick Vujicic could have easily succumbed to despair and self-pity. However, he chose a different path. Nick embraced gratitude for the abilities he did have and focused on living a purposeful life. He became an inspirational speaker, spreading a message of hope and gratitude to millions around the world, reminding them of the power of a grateful mindset.

4. *Anne Frank:* Anne Frank, a Jewish girl hiding from the Nazis during World War II, demonstrated remarkable gratitude despite the dire circumstances. Her diary, which she kept while in hiding, is filled with expressions of gratitude for the beauty of nature, the kindness of others, and the joy she found in simple moments. Anne's gratitude amidst unimaginable hardship serves as a testament to the resilience of the human spirit. Anne consistently expressed her love and appreciation for her family, particularly her father, Otto Frank. She often wrote about her close relationship with her father and her gratitude for his guidance and support. Despite the difficult circumstances

of hiding in a concealed annex, Anne expressed gratitude for having a place to hide from the Nazis. She recognized that being in hiding was a lifeline for her and her family, as it protected them from immediate danger. Throughout her diary, Anne maintained hope for a better future. She believed in the goodness of humanity and expressed gratitude for the possibility of a world where people would understand each other better and live in peace.

5. *John F. Kennedy:* John F. Kennedy, the 35th President of the United States, faced numerous challenges during his presidency, including the Cuban Missile Crisis and civil rights struggles. Despite these trials, he often encouraged the nation to be grateful for the blessings of freedom, democracy, and the potential for progress. Kennedy's gratitude in the face of adversity served as a source of inspiration for the American people during tumultuous times. During the Cold War, Kennedy valued and expressed gratitude for the support and solidarity of America's allies in countering the threat of communism. He understood the importance of international cooperation and alliance-building.

These individuals remind us that gratitude is not dependent on external circumstances but a choice we can make regardless of our challenges. Their examples demonstrate the transformative power of gratitude in fostering resilience, inspiring others, and finding meaning even in the most challenging times.

Barriers to Gratitude in Hard Times

Gratitude can be challenging to cultivate during hard times due to several barriers and obstacles that individuals may face.

a. *Despair and Hopelessness:* Losing sight of God's promises can plunge us into despair, clouding our ability to see His blessings.

b. *Isolation:* Withdrawing from the community can deprive us of much-needed support and encouragement.

c. *Bitterness and Resentment:* Harboring anger towards God or others can stifle gratitude.

d. *Comparison:* Weighing our suffering against that of others can either breed pride or self-pity, both of which are detrimental to a grateful heart.

Steps for giving thanks in adversity:

1. Reframe Perspective:

Shift Focus: Every situation, no matter how bleak, has some positive elements. Instead of being consumed by the negative, intentionally search for and focus on the positive. For example, one might find closer connections with loved ones during an illness.

Seek Growth: Adversity often acts as a catalyst for personal growth. You may discover newfound strength, resilience, or understanding by asking yourself what lessons the situation is teaching you.

2. Remember Past Triumphs:

By recalling moments when you faced and overcame challenges in the past, you're reminding yourself of your inherent resilience and capability. These memories serve as personal touchstones of strength and indicate that current adversities will pass.

3. Seek Support:

When you open up to trusted friends or family, they might bring attention to aspects of the situation you hadn't noticed or offer reminders of your strengths and blessings. Being heard can, in itself, be therapeutic and a source of gratitude.

4. Connect with Faith:

Prayer, meditation, or any spiritual practice can create a space where you're reminded of a greater narrative or divine plan. Faith offers hope and a renewed perspective, allowing you to see beyond the immediate adversity.

5. Engage in Acts of Kindness:

Giving, even in the simplest of ways, can bring a sense of purpose and satisfaction. Whether it's a smile, a kind word, or a charitable act, these gestures can provide a tangible feeling of interconnectedness and gratitude.

6. Limit Exposure to Negativity:

Consistently consuming negative information can skew your perspective. Finding a balance, like setting aside specific times to check the news or limiting exposure to pessimistic conversations, can help maintain a more grateful mindset.

7. Celebrate Small Wins:

Acknowledging even minor triumphs builds momentum for gratitude. Did you manage a difficult conversation? Find a moment of peace on a tough day. Recognize and celebrate these moments.

8. Seek Inspiration:

Stories of resilience, whether from literature, history, or personal anecdotes, can inspire gratitude. They testify that humans have an innate capacity to find and express gratitude, even in the face of significant challenges.

9. Be Patient with Yourself:

Gratitude in adversity isn't about ignoring pain or forcing positivity. It's about recognizing the spectrum of human experience. Some days will be more challenging than others, and it's essential to acknowledge your feelings without judgment.

10. Embracing the Full Spectrum of Life

Life, in all its complexity, comprises both sunshine and shadows. Embracing both with a heart of gratitude is not merely an act of defiance against adversity but a profound affirmation of faith. As believers, we're called to navigate every season with a heart anchored in gratitude, finding an opportunity for deeper spiritual growth and understanding in every circumstance.

CHAPTER'S REFLECTION

- An important component of Christian faith and practice is being grateful in the midst of difficulties and challenges. Even though it may seem contradictory to be thankful amid trying times, the Bible and Christian teachings emphasize the importance of a thankful attitude no matter the situation.

- There are both biblical and contemporary examples of people whose reaction to adversity was gratitude. If they could do it, we can do it too!

Gratitude in Times of Abundance

04

In this chapter, we will explore the fascinating concept of gratitude in times of abundance. We often assume gratitude naturally follows when life is filled with blessings and success. However, prosperity and abundance can sometimes hinder our ability to truly appreciate and be grateful for what we have.

Gratitude in times of abundance is a fundamental Christian principle that centers on recognizing and appreciating God's blessings, even when one's life is filled with plenty and prosperity. It is rooted in the belief that every good gift and blessing comes from God, and Christians are encouraged to maintain an attitude of gratitude regardless of their circumstances.

This chapter will provide insights on maintaining a grateful mindset amidst blessings and success, drawing from biblical teachings on stewardship and using abundance to bless others.

The Hidden Challenges of Abundance:

Prosperity and abundance come with their own set of

challenges regarding gratitude. It is easy to become complacent or take things for granted when everything seems to be going well. We may become focused on acquiring more material possessions or achieving higher levels of success rather than appreciating and being grateful for what we already have. Recognizing these challenges and consciously cultivating gratitude in our lives is essential.

The word "abundance" brings forth images of plenty—food, gadgets, entertainment, opportunities, and more. Our contemporary age is replete with innovations and conveniences our ancestors couldn't have imagined. Smartphones offer global communication in the palm of our hands. Online platforms provide instant access to education, entertainment, and social connections. Supermarkets overflow with a wide array of food items from across the globe. In short, for many, there is no dearth of material pleasures.

However, this surplus often breeds a feeling of overwhelm. The parable of "the paradox of choice" illustrates that individuals often feel paralyzed when presented with numerous choices instead of feeling liberated. This overabundance can lead to decision fatigue, making us less likely to appreciate our decisions or the many opportunities available.

For instance, streaming platforms with thousands of shows

and movies can sometimes lead to hours of browsing without ever settling on one, resulting in the ironic feeling that there's nothing to watch in a sea of options.

With abundance often comes the relentless chase for the "new." In a consumer-driven society, the next model, upgrade, or trend is always on the horizon. The constant barrage of advertising and social media feeds fosters an environment where what one has now seems insufficient compared to the next best thing. This diminishes the intrinsic value of what's already possessed, making gratitude a fleeting emotion.

The digital age, particularly the rise of social media, has also fueled an unprecedented culture of comparison. People are perpetually exposed to curated highlights of others' lives, leading to feelings of inadequacy. It's challenging to be grateful for one's circumstances when juxtaposed with seemingly 'perfect' lives, even if those portrayals are often far from the complete truth.

The Danger

In the Gospel of Luke, Jesus presents a compelling narrative about a prosperous man intoxicated by his material affluence, becoming heedless of life's more significant meanings and spiritual truths. The parable of the Rich Fool (Luke 12:13-21) offers a timeless message about the danger of ingratitude, particularly during times of abundance.

Then one from the crowd said to Him, "Teacher, tell my brother to divide the inheritance with me."

But He said to him, "Man, who made Me a judge or an arbitrator over you?" And He said to them, "Take heed and beware of covetousness, for one's life does not consist in the abundance of the things he possesses."

Then He spoke a parable to them, saying: "The ground of a certain rich man yielded plentifully. And he thought within himself, saying, "What shall I do, since I have no room to store my crops?' So he said, 'I will do this: I will pull down my barns and build greater, and there I will store all my crops and my goods. And I will say to my soul, "Soul, you have many goods laid up for many years; take your ease; eat, drink, and be merry."' But God said to him, 'Fool! This night your soul will be required of you; then whose will those things be which you have provided?'

Luke 12:13-21
"So is he who lays up treasure for himself, and is not rich toward God."

Amidst a gathering, a man approaches Jesus, imploring him to arbitrate an inheritance dispute. Rather than getting entangled in material contention, Jesus uses the opportunity to share a cautionary tale, urging the audience to guard against all forms of greed and ingratitude.

The parable tells of a wealthy farmer whose lands produced plentiful crops. Instead of being grateful for his blessing, the farmer's thoughts revolve around how to hoard his surplus. He plans to tear down his barns to build larger ones, ensuring he can store all his grain and goods.

The farmer finds comfort in his amassed wealth, believing it guarantees his future. "Soul, you have many goods laid up for many years; take your ease; eat, drink, and be merry," he tells himself, confident in his self-made security. Yet his trust in his wealth blinds him from recognizing life's unpredictability and the transient nature of earthly possessions.

God intervenes, declaring, "Fool! This night your soul will be required of you; then whose will those things be which you have provided?" The farmer's life comes to an unforeseen end, and he cannot take his treasures with him. His ingratitude and misplaced priorities led to an eternal loss.

Lessons Here

- The farmer's fundamental mistake was overlooking the source of his prosperity. His lands were fertile, not by his merit alone but by God's grace. In times of abundance, it's easy to forget the divine providence or the collaborative efforts that lead to success, resulting in ingratitude.

- The farmer believed he was securing his future by relying solely on his wealth. However, life's uncertainties remain beyond our control. Ingratitude arises when we falsely think we're entirely self-sufficient, dismissing external aids and blessings.

- The farmer prioritized material accumulation over spiritual and relational wealth. When consumed by materialism, it's easy to neglect relationships, virtues, and spiritual growth. An ungrateful heart often sidelines what truly matters.

Cultivating Gratitude in Times of Abundance

Psalm 103:1-2 says:
"Bless the Lord, O my soul; and all that is within me, bless his holy name. Bless the Lord, O my soul, and forget not all his benefits."

At its core, this Psalm is a heartfelt song of gratitude to God. It reminds us to pause, reflect, and give thanks for the many blessings we have received. It's easy to forget the countless benefits and blessings in times of plenty, but this passage challenges us to actively remember them.

1. **Total Gratitude**: The phrase "Bless the Lord, O my soul; and all that is within me" evokes an image of complete and overwhelming gratitude. This is not just a passing thank you

but a deep, soul-stirring appreciation that encompasses our entire being. In times of plenty, we are encouraged to engage in this level of thankfulness, acknowledging both the material blessings and the deeper spiritual ones.

2. **An Active Reminder**: The line, "and forget not all his benefits," encourages mindfulness. In the abundance of our modern lives, it's easy to take our blessings for granted. But, as the Psalm suggests, we should always remember the source of our prosperity. Every good gift, every joy, and even the very air we breathe can be traced back to God.

3. **More than Material**: While focusing on the material blessings in times of plenty is easy, the Psalm invites us to recognize the intangible benefits. These might include peace of mind, love, joy, patience, and other fruits of the spirit. These often overlooked gifts are just as, if not more, valuable than material possessions.

In the hustle and bustle of prosperous times, remaining grounded in gratitude is a challenge. Yet, Psalm 103:1-5 serves as a poignant reminder to keep our hearts and minds centered on thankfulness. The passage calls us to recognize, with all our heart and soul, the abundant blessings poured out upon us.

Bless the Lord, O my soul;
And all that is within me, bless His holy name!
Bless the Lord, O my soul,
And forget not all His benefits:

Who forgives all your iniquities,
Who heals all your diseases,
Who redeems your life from destruction,
Who crowns you with lovingkindness and tender mercies,
Who satisfies your mouth with good things,
So that your youth is renewed like the eagle's.
Psalm 103:1-5 (NKJV)

Let us remember that gratitude in times of plenty is just as crucial as in times of scarcity. It aligns our spirit with God, keeping us humble, grounded, and ever-aware of the benevolence that fills our lives. By heeding the call of Psalm 103:1-5, we can nurture a heart that sings with gratitude, no matter the season of our lives. Top of Form

Shifting Our Perspective

One key principle in maintaining gratitude amidst abundance is shifting our perspective from scarcity to abundance. Instead of focusing on what we lack, we can focus on the abundance surrounding us. This shift in mindset opens our eyes to the blessings we often overlook.

Also, taking time each day to count our blessings is a powerful practice that reinforces gratitude. Whether through journaling, creating a gratitude jar, or simply reflecting on the day's blessings, this practice keeps us attuned to the abundance in our lives.

In Exodus 16, after escaping Egypt, the Israelites found themselves in the desert, hungry and discontent. God provided them with manna, a miraculous food source that appeared daily. However, they were instructed to gather only what they needed each day (except for the Sabbath). This was a lesson in reliance on God and appreciating daily blessings without hoarding or indulgence.

Then the Lord said to Moses, "Behold, I will rain bread from heaven for you. And the people shall go out and gather a certain quota every day, that I may test them, whether they will walk in My law or not. And it shall be on the sixth day that they shall prepare what they bring in, and it shall be twice as much as they gather daily."

So it was that quail came up at evening and covered the camp, and in the morning the dew lay all around the camp. And when the layer of dew lifted, there, on the surface of the wilderness, was a small round substance, as fine as frost on the ground. So when the children of Israel saw it, they said to one another, "What is it?" For they did not know what it was.

And Moses said to them, "This is the bread which the Lord has given you to eat. This is the thing which the Lord has commanded: 'Let every man gather it according to each one's need, one omer for each person, according to the number of persons; let every man take for those who are in his tent." **Exodus 16:4-5, 13-16 (NKJV)**

After building a grand temple, King Solomon offered a prayer of gratitude: "Blessed be the Lord, who has given rest to his people Israel according to all that he promised. Not one word has failed of all his good promise." Even amidst the temple's grandeur, Solomon focused on God's faithfulness.

Blessed be the Lord, who has given rest to His people Israel, according to all that He promised. There has not failed one word of all His good promise, which He promised through His servant Moses. May the Lord our God be with us, as He was with our fathers. May He not leave us nor forsake us, that He may incline our hearts to Himself, to walk in all His ways, and to keep His commandments and His statutes and His judgments, which He commanded our fathers. And may these words of mine, with which I have made supplication before the Lord, be near the Lord our God day and night, that He may maintain the cause of His servant and the cause of His people Israel, as each day may require, that all the peoples of the earth may know that the Lord is God; there is no other. Let your heart therefore be loyal to the Lord our God, to walk in His statutes and keep His commandments, as at this day. **1 Kings 8:56-61 (NKJV)**

John was an individual who had achieved great financial success. However, he found himself constantly chasing after more wealth and possessions, never feeling satisfied or grateful for what he had. Recognizing the negative impact this was having on his well-being, John decided to embark on a gratitude journey. He started by practicing mindfulness and being present in the moment, appreciating the small things that brought him joy. He also made a conscious effort to give back to the community by volunteering at a local shelter and donating a portion of his income to causes he cared about. Over time, John realized that true abundance and fulfillment came not from material possessions but from cultivating a mindset of gratitude and using his blessings to make a positive impact. Through his journey, John found greater contentment and peace and inspired those around him to embrace gratitude and live with a sense of purpose.

Maintaining gratitude in times of abundance is a transformative journey that requires conscious effort and a shift in perspective. By recognizing the challenges that come with abundance, cultivating gratitude through mindfulness and counting our blessings, embracing biblical teachings on stewardship, and implementing practical tips, we can navigate the complexities of abundance with grace and humility. Let us assume the power of gratitude and unlock the extraordinary blessings that await in times of plenty.

CHAPTER'S REFLECTION

- Gratitude in times of abundance in the Christian context is about recognizing God's blessings, being good stewards of those blessings, finding contentment in His provision, and demonstrating love and generosity toward others. It is an expression of faith, humility, and thanksgiving, serving as a reminder that all blessings ultimately come from God and should be used to glorify Him and benefit humanity.

- Gratitude in times of abundance is often accompanied by a sense of responsibility. We are called to be good stewards of the blessings we have received, using our resources wisely and generously to help others and advance God's kingdom.

- Gratitude is grounded in humility; as Christians, we must acknowledge our dependence on God and the temporary nature of material possessions.

The Role of Gratitude in Worship

05

G ratitude and worship are inextricably linked, each amplifying the essence of the other. Gratitude plays a significant role in Christian worship and is deeply embedded in the faith's spiritual practices and teachings. When we approach God with hearts filled with genuine appreciation, it becomes a profound acknowledgment of His sovereignty and ever-present goodness in our lives.

This chapter delves into this sacred relationship, exploring the depth and breadth of gratitude's role in worship and prayer.

1. Psalms and Hymns of Gratitude:

Throughout the scriptures, psalms and hymns have played a crucial role in worship, echoing the sentiments of the human heart towards its Creator. Their words often encapsulate the essence of gratitude, urging the believer to approach God with songs of thanksgiving.

Psalm 95:2 says, "*Let us come before him with thanksgiving and extol him with music and song.*"This verse not only signifies the importance of music in worship but also emphasizes the attitude of gratitude that should accompany it. Many Christian worship songs and hymns also contain themes of gratitude and thanksgiving. These songs encourage congregants to express their thankfulness to God for His love, mercy, and salvation. Singing praises and offering thanks is a common practice in Christian worship.

2. The Communal Aspect of Grateful Worship:

Worship is not just an individual act; it is a collective experience that binds believers in unity. When communities come together in gratitude, they amplify their voices in unison, forming a harmonious symphony of praise.

Colossians 3:16 implores, *"Let the message of Christ dwell among you richly as you teach and admonish one another with all wisdom through psalms, hymns, and songs from the Spirit, singing to God with gratitude in your hearts."* Here, the emphasis is on the collective spirit of grateful worship.

3. Physical Expressions of Gratitude in Worship:

Worship often transcends verbal expression. The physical acts—whether kneeling, raising hands, or lying prostrate—speak volumes of a heart's gratitude. These actions, done in reverence and love, further deepen the intimacy of our worship.

Psalm 95:6 beckons, *"Come, let us bow down in worship, let us kneel before the Lord our Maker."* The posture not only showcases humility but also profound gratitude towards our Creator.

Gratitude in Prayer

1. The Lord's Prayer:

Christ's lesson on prayer was not just a set of words to repeat but a blueprint for approaching God. Embedded in it is the essence of gratitude, acknowledging God's daily provision and the coming of His kingdom.

Delving into Matthew 6:9-13, we see the framework of grateful acknowledgment, especially in the phrase, *"Give us this day our daily bread."*

2. Intercessory Prayers with Gratitude:

Praying for others, or intercession, is a beautiful act of love. When this is done with a spirit of gratitude, recognizing God's work in their lives, it amplifies the power of the prayer.

In Philippians 1:3-4, Paul exclaims, "I thank my God every time I remember you. In all my prayers for all of you, I always pray with joy." This intertwining of intercession and gratitude showcases a heart that's deeply connected to God's people.

3. Gratitude in Personal Petitions:

While making personal requests to God, it's important to do so with a heart filled with gratitude. This displays our trust in His plan and His inherent goodness.

Philippians 4:6 advises, *"Do not be anxious about anything, but in every situation, by prayer and petition, with thanksgiving, present your requests to God."* This scripture underscores the importance of pairing our petitions with gratitude.

Worship and Prayer

When gratitude becomes the underpinning of our worship and prayer, it can transform our spiritual life and every facet of our existence. Such gratitude-driven spiritual practices usher in divine interventions, spiritual breakthroughs, and an unparalleled intimacy with God.

Crafting a Grateful Spiritual Discipline

Incorporating gratitude into our spiritual regimen doesn't just enrich our relationship with God; it crafts a life that resonates with joy, peace, and fulfillment. By keeping a gratitude journal, dedicating special days for thanksgiving prayers, and emphasizing hymns of gratitude in worship, we can ensure that our hearts are always attuned to the countless blessings showered upon us.

Gratitude in worship and prayer isn't just an act; it's a lifestyle, a conscious choice to recognize and honor God's ceaseless love and abundant provisions. As we navigate our spiritual journey, let's ensure that gratitude remains our steadfast companion, guiding and enriching our path.

The Power of Thanksgiving

In the Christian faith, thanksgiving holds a special place of significance. From the earliest days of the Israelites to the teachings of Jesus Christ and the writings of the Apostles, giving thanks to God resonates throughout scripture as a powerful spiritual discipline. This attitude of gratitude not only builds personal character but also unleashes divine favor and intervention.

Though David did not build the temple himself, he made extensive preparations for its construction and expressed profound gratitude for the opportunity to play a part in its establishment. In 1 Chronicles 29:10-14, David offers a beautiful prayer of thanksgiving. He says:

"Praise be to you, LORD, the God of our father Israel, from everlasting to everlasting. Yours, LORD, is the greatness and the power and the glory and the majesty and the splendor, for everything in heaven and earth is yours. Yours, LORD, is the kingdom; you are exalted as head over all. Wealth and honor come from you; you are the ruler of all things. In your hands are strength and power to exalt and give strength to all. Now, our God, we give you thanks, and praise your glorious name."

David's heart was filled with gratitude and awe for God's

greatness, acknowledging that everything comes from Him.

A dramatic example of the power of thanksgiving in the face of adversity is the story of King Jehoshaphat in 2 Chronicles 20. He sought the Lord's guidance when the Moabites and Ammonites came to wage war against Jehoshaphat. After receiving a word from the Lord through Jahaziel, Jehoshaphat appointed men to sing to the Lord and praise him for the splendor of his holiness as they went out at the head of the army. They sang:

"Give thanks to the LORD, for his love endures forever."

As they began to sing and praise, the Lord set ambushes against the men of Ammon, Moab, and Mount Seir, who were invading Judah, and they were defeated. Here, thanksgiving was not a mere acknowledgment but a weapon of warfare.

Insights into Thanksgiving

1. An Act of Faith:

Thanksgiving, especially during challenging times, is an act of faith. It is a declaration that God is sovereign, in control, and working all things for the good of those who love Him. *"And we know that all things work together for good to them that love God, to them who are the called according to his purpose"* (Romans 8:28).

2. Entering God's Presence:

Psalm 100:4 states: *"Enter his gates with thanksgiving and his courts with praise; give thanks to him and praise his name."*

Thanksgiving is a means by which believers approach God, signifying that gratitude is a precursor to deeper intimacy and fellowship with Him.

3. A Guard Against Discontent:

In Philippians 4:6, Apostle Paul advises:

"Do not be anxious about anything, but in every situation, by prayer and petition, with thanksgiving, present your requests to God."

By coupling prayer with thanksgiving, believers are reminded to maintain a perspective that sees God's goodness, which guards the heart from discontent and anxiety.

4. It's God's Will:

1 Thessalonians 5:18 says, *"Give thanks in all circumstances; for this is God's will for you in Christ Jesus."* Thanksgiving is not just a suggestion; it's God's will for every believer.

Thanksgiving can shift our focus from our problems to God's promises. It can break the chains of worry, lift the weight of burden, and usher in peace. When gratitude fills the heart, there's less room for doubt, fear, and negativity.

Challenges and Misconceptions

While the pursuit of gratitude is virtuous, it's essential to recognize that there can be challenges and misconceptions along the way:

Overcompensation: There's a fine line between genuine gratitude and forcing positive thinking. It's okay to acknowledge pain, sadness, or disappointment; gratitude isn't about denying negative emotions but about finding a balanced perspective.

Comparative Gratitude: Avoid the trap of thinking, "I should be grateful because others have it worse." While perspective can be beneficial, true gratitude comes from genuine appreciation, not comparison.

Avoiding Complacency: Being grateful for what you have doesn't mean you shouldn't aspire for growth or change. It's about appreciating the journey and the present moment, even as you aim for new horizons.

Gratitude as a Lifelong Journey

Cultivating a mindset of gratitude is not a one-time act but a lifelong journey. It's akin to tending a garden; regular care, attention, and reflection help the seeds of gratitude sprout, grow, and flourish.

Our world, with its emphasis on acquisition and achievement, can often cloud our vision, making it difficult to see the already present blessings. But by consciously practicing gratitude, we can bring clarity to our perspective, enriching our lives and the lives of those around us.

Gratitude is more than just a positive emotion—it's a mindset, a way of life. By focusing on the good, acknowledging the blessings in our lives, and expressing our appreciation, we can lead happier, more fulfilled lives. As the saying goes, "It's not happiness that brings us gratitude. It's gratitude that brings us happiness." Embrace this philosophy, cultivate this mindset, and witness the transformative power of gratitude.

CHAPTER'S REFLECTION

- Gratitude is a fundamental and pervasive element of Christian worship. It permeates prayers, rituals, songs, and teachings, reminding believers to acknowledge God's goodness, offer thanks for His blessings, and live out their faith with a grateful heart.

- Gratitude is not only an integral part of worship but also a way of life for Christians, influencing their interactions with God and others.

Laws of
Gratitude

06

Gratitude and God's Laws

Gratitude, while being a deep emotional response, is also intricately woven into the fabric of God's laws. These laws are not merely rules to be obeyed; they are principles that guide our spiritual growth, deepen our relationship with God, and enhance our understanding of life. By delving into these laws, we see how gratitude is not just an act but aligns with God's principles for a fulfilled life.

Law 1: The Law of Reciprocity

This law illustrates the powerful dynamic of give and take, suggesting that what we extend into the world, be it gratitude, kindness, or love, finds its way back to us, often multiplied.

Central to this law is the concept of heartfelt gratitude. Gratitude isn't a mere sentiment or fleeting feeling. It is an active acknowledgment of the blessings we've received, both big and small. When we actively show our appreciation, it acts as a magnet, drawing more good into our lives. It is as though the universe responds to our thankful hearts by saying, "You appreciate this? Let me give you more."

Luke 6:38 encapsulates this idea perfectly: "Give, and it will be given to you." While this biblical passage can be interpreted in various ways, its relevance to The Law of Reciprocity is evident. By generously expressing our gratitude, especially towards God, we are not only recognizing the good that we currently possess but also creating space for more blessings to flow into our lives.

In essence, The Law of Reciprocity is a testament to the interconnectedness of all things. By understanding and practicing it, we enhance our personal lives and contribute positively to the greater good. The more we sincerely appreciate, the more we prepare ourselves to be vessels of receiving, creating a virtuous cycle of blessings and gratitude.

By expressing our gratitude, especially towards God, we inherently position ourselves to receive His endless blessings.

Law 2: Law of Worship

In understanding the spiritual realm, one often encounters principles that define the relationship between the divine and the mortal. Among these, The Law of Worship stands prominent, emphasizing that genuine worship transcends mere rituals and practices. It instead calls upon a profound connection with God, rooted deeply in gratitude.

True worship isn't limited to singing hymns, reciting prayers, or even attending religious ceremonies. While these acts are necessary and can be expressions of our devotion, they are merely external manifestations. The essence of worship lies in the heart's orientation. A heart steeped in gratitude resonates at a frequency that aligns with divine realities. Such a heart recognizes the benevolence of the Almighty in every facet of life—in challenges as much as in blessings.

For instance, think of when a woman rises to share her testimony during a silent moment in a service. She speaks not of the hymns sung or the sermon preached but of the inexplicable peace she felt during a personal crisis, expressing deep gratitude for that divine solace. Her words are raw, genuine, and rooted in appreciation— that's true worship.

Psalm 100:4 is a beautiful reminder of this sentiment. "Enter his gates with thanksgiving and his courts with praise." This scripture isn't merely an instruction; it's an insight into the nature of divine communion. Entering the 'gates' and 'courts' symbolizes approaching the divine presence. And how should one approach it? With thanksgiving—an acknowledgment of God's benevolence and mercy. This scripture underscores that gratitude isn't just an afterthought but the foundation of true worship.

For example, a man who has faced a year of challenges—job loss, health issues, and personal setbacks. Yet, every night, he kneels by his bedside, not asking for reprieve but expressing gratitude for the strength he's been given to endure. This daily ritual is more than a habit; it's an act of worship, recognizing God's hand even in adversity.

To truly worship, then, is to continuously live with a heart full of gratitude. It's about seeing God's hand in the tapestry of our life experiences and acknowledging it with genuine appreciation. In doing so, we draw closer to God and enrich our spiritual journey.

In essence, true worship is akin to a child who, after receiving a gift, rushes not to play with it but first to hug the giver in sheer appreciation. It's about recognizing and cherishing the source of our blessings, both big and small, and responding with heartfelt gratitude. This is the crux of The Law of Worship.

Law 3: The Law of Humility

In the journey of life, The Law of Humility serves as a crucial compass, guiding our interactions, emotions, and perspectives. At its core, this law underscores the importance of gratitude as the grounding force. Every human, irrespective of their status, wealth, or intelligence, has inherent limitations. These limitations are a stark reminder of our frailties and vulnerabilities, and the realization of this truth breeds humility.

Gratitude is not just an emotion; it's a state of being. When we are grateful, we acknowledge the blessings, big and small, that permeate our lives. This acknowledgment brings us joy and centers us, ensuring that we do not become too boastful or overly confident in our capabilities. When we take a moment to reflect on the many instances where circumstances could have been otherwise, it reinforces our reliance on a power greater than ours. For many, this higher power is God.

James 4:6 offers a profound insight into the spiritual significance of humility: "God opposes the proud but shows favor to the humble." This scripture emphasizes that pride can alienate us from God. When we operate from a place of pride, we often close our eyes to our shortcomings and, inadvertently, to God's interventions in our lives. In contrast, humility brings us closer to God, fostering a deeper connection and understanding of His workings.

Seeing God's influence in every aspect of our lives is essential, even in the seemingly mundane. For instance, consider the opportunities and relationships that have shaped us. While it's easy to attribute our successes solely to our hard work or talents, recognizing that many factors, some beyond our comprehension, played a role fosters humility.

Imagine a talented pianist who, while talented, happened to have a teacher in her youth who recognized and nurtured her potential. The intersection of her innate talent, her teacher's guidance, and the countless hours of practice led her to success. Recognizing this interconnectedness and God's role in orchestrating these encounters instills humility and gratitude.

The Law of Humility teaches us that gratitude is not just a

fleeting emotion but a continuous practice. It aligns our hearts and minds, making us more receptive to divine interventions, fostering humility, and deepening our bond with God.

Law 4: The Law of Reflection

Life can often be a whirlwind of activities, duties, and distractions. Amidst this chaos, The Law of Reflection emerges as a beacon, urging individuals to pause and reflect. This law is not scientific but spiritual. It emphasizes the importance of reminiscing and acknowledging the wonders of God in our lives.

The Law of Reflection is profoundly rooted in scripture, particularly in Psalm 77:11, which states, "I will remember the deeds of the LORD." The very act of recalling God's mercies and blessings isn't merely an exercise in nostalgia. It is a transformative action that bolsters our spirits, reinforces our faith, and magnifies our sense of gratitude.

By engaging in this reflective practice, we deepen our understanding of God's grace and find the strength to face challenges with renewed vigor. It provides an anchor, grounding us when we feel adrift and offering solace in times of turmoil. When we recall moments when God's presence was palpable in our lives, our hearts swell with gratitude, and our bond with God is further cemented.

Consider a person who has faced numerous challenges throughout the year—health concerns, financial difficulties, or personal losses. Amidst the shadows of these trials, it's easy for this individual to feel overwhelmed. However, by adhering to The Law of Reflection and taking a moment to remember the times God intervened—either by providing strength, sending help, or opening new doors—this individual can rejuvenate their spirit and approach the future with hope.

Imagine a young woman at a crossroads in her life, uncertain of her chosen path. Instead of succumbing to anxiety, she reflects on past instances where God's guidance was evident in her life. Perhaps it was a chance encounter that led to a job opportunity or an unexpected source of support during a trying time. By recollecting these divine interventions, she is reminded that she is not alone in her journey and is encouraged to trust in God's plan for her future.

Therefore, The Law of Reflection isn't just about retrospection. It is a spiritual tool that offers clarity and instills profound gratitude. By making it a habit to reflect on God's blessings, we enrich our spiritual journey and nurture a resilient and grateful heart.

Law 5: The Law of Contentment

Being truly grateful means finding contentment in our present circumstances. Such contentment does not arise from complacency but from an unwavering faith and belief that our lives are intricately designed and that God always provides precisely what we need. In a world driven by aspirations, desires, and often an unquenchable thirst for more, it's easy to overlook the blessings we already have and to become entrapped in a cycle of wanting more.

Scripture provides profound wisdom on the topic. In Philippians 4:11-12, Paul addresses this very sentiment. He writes, "Not that I speak in regard to need, for I have learned in whatever state I am, to be content: I know how to be abased, and I know how to abound. Everywhere and in all things, I have learned both to be full and to be hungry, both to abound and to suffer need." These words suggest that contentment isn't about having everything but finding peace in whatever we have. Paul's contentment springs from a heart full of gratitude and a realization that there's a purpose, a design, and a loving God overseeing it all, in abundance or lack.

Consider a man living in a small apartment with just enough to get by. While many around him aspire for bigger homes and fancier cars, he finds peace and happiness in his humble abode. It's not that he doesn't have dreams or aspirations, but he understands the value of what he has: a roof over his head, food on the table, and the love of his family. His gratitude for these essentials allows him to be content, knowing that he has what he truly needs in this moment.

Having faced multiple setbacks in her career, a woman remains positive and content. Rather than becoming bitter or envious of her peers who might be scaling professional heights, she finds gratitude in the lessons learned from each setback. She believes that God has a unique path for her, and these experiences are shaping her for a bigger purpose. Her contentment stems not from external achievements but from an inner peace, knowing that she is exactly where she needs to be.

In conclusion, The Law of Contentment serves as a reminder that gratitude and contentment are closely intertwined. In recognizing and appreciating our present blessings, we pave the way for a life filled with joy and fulfillment, grounded in the belief that God's provisions are always just right for us.

Law 6: The Law of Sowing and Reaping

The Law of Sowing and Reaping is an enduring and universal principle that governs every aspect of our lives. At its heart, this law underscores a profound truth: the energy, intentions, and actions we put forth today are directly proportional to the outcomes we receive tomorrow. The principle is simple yet potent: we will eventually reap what we nurture and sow.

In a spiritual and emotional context, when we talk about sowing, it doesn't necessarily mean planting tangible seeds in the soil. Instead, it refers to the investments we make in our character, the attitudes we adopt, the relationships we cultivate, and especially the gratitude we express. When we sow seeds of kindness, love, generosity, and gratitude, we cultivate a life filled with abundant blessings and positive returns.

2 Corinthians 9:6 articulates this law perfectly: "Whoever sows sparingly will also reap sparingly, and whoever sows generously will also reap generously." The scripture accentuates the importance of our offerings, especially in gratitude. When we openly and generously express gratitude, we open doors to an abundance of blessings in our spiritual and emotional lives.

Imagine a person who consistently sows seeds of bitterness, resentment, and negativity. Over time, these seeds grow into thorny bushes in their hearts, strangling joy and peace. Their relationships suffer, they find it difficult to experience happiness, and they may even feel isolated. This is the harvest of what they've sown.

On the contrary, take another individual who always seeks to find the good in situations, expresses thankfulness in both times of prosperity and adversity, and consistently nurtures their relationships with love and understanding. Over time, this person reaps a harvest of joy, peace, deeper relationships, and an enriched spiritual life.

There were two examples of coworkers. One always complained, seldom acknowledging the help of others. The other, however, often expressed gratitude, celebrated team successes, and acknowledged the efforts of colleagues. Over time, the latter reaped the benefits of stronger relationships, trust, and likely more opportunities, while the former may have found himself isolated.

In conclusion, The Law of Sowing and Reaping is a potent reminder that our present actions and attitudes directly affect our future outcomes. Sowing generously, especially in terms of gratitude, ensures an abundant harvest in our spiritual and emotional lives.

Law 7: The Law of Purity

In the spiritual and emotional growth journey, The Law of Purity stands as a beacon of inner transformation. The essence of this law revolves around the concept that a heart filled to the brim with gratitude will inherently repel negative emotions and afflictions like envy, greed, and discontent. When gratitude becomes the cornerstone of one's emotional and spiritual foundation, there is little room for these toxic feelings to take root and flourish.

The words from Matthew 5:8 echo this sentiment, stating, "Blessed are the pure in heart, for they will see God." This verse conveys the notion that purity of heart, exemplified by an attitude of thankfulness, is not just about experiencing peace and contentment. It is about achieving a deeper, divine connection, allowing one to truly "see" and experience God in every nuance of life.

Consider a person named Sarah. She had always been competitive and constantly compared her life to those around her. Her friend bought a new car, and she felt pangs of envy, wondering why she couldn't afford one. Another friend got promoted, and she was consumed with jealousy. However, a transformation occurred when Sarah started to practice gratitude daily, reflecting on the blessings she had rather than what she lacked. Instead of envy, she felt joy for her friends. Instead of feeling discontent with her life, she celebrated the small joys and realized she was surrounded by blessings. Her heart, now grateful, felt a deeper connection with God.

Mike was a successful businessman. His insatiable greed for more made him lose friends and family along the way. One day, after a close brush with death, he began to count his blessings, realizing the fragility of life. His heart became full of gratitude for each day, for every relationship, and for all the simple joys. The greed that once consumed him started to diminish. In its place grew a heart of service, and he found himself more connected to God, experiencing the profoundness of life's every moment.

In conclusion, The Law of Purity emphasizes the transformative power of gratitude. When we allow gratitude to purify our hearts, we not only dispel negative emotions but also usher in a profound connection with our heavenly Father. Embracing this law can pave the way for a life enriched with spiritual depth and emotional freedom.

Gratitude: A Divine Principle

The Biblical laws of gratitude provide a roadmap for a spiritually enriching life. Aligning with these principles not only cultivates a heart of thanksgiving but also deepens our communion with God.

As we navigate life, keeping these laws at the forefront ensures our journey is not only guided by gratitude but also in harmony with God's divine intent for our lives.

The scriptures are replete with wisdom on gratitude, painting it not merely as an emotion but as a divine principle. These seven biblical laws shed light on the multifaceted nature of gratitude, urging us to embrace it in moments of joy and as a perpetual spiritual practice. Doing so enriches our lives and walks in step with God's design.

Applications and Reflections

It's one thing to understand these laws and another to integrate them into our daily lives. Each law invites us to reflect on our relationship with God, others, and ourselves.

Practicing The Law of Reciprocity can start as simply as voicing our thanks for daily provisions. This gratitude in acknowledgment invites more of God's grace into our lives.

The Law of Worship emphasizes the idea that our every action can be an act of worship if approached with a heart full of gratitude. Whether through our jobs, interactions with others, or daily chores, acknowledging God's presence in these acts can transform the mundane into sacred moments of worship.

Living out The Law of Humility requires regular self-reflection. Recognizing that every achievement, no matter how personal, has a divine touch to it helps keep our pride at bay.

Embracing The Law of Reflection, one might make it a routine to end the day by recounting at least three ways God manifested in their life. This simple act can instill a deeper sense of gratitude.

Contentment in today's material world can seem challenging. Yet, it's essential for our spiritual and emotional well-being. The Law of Contentment prompts us to cherish what we have, finding joy in the little things.

To reap the blessings of gratitude, we need to sow it generously in our lives. This means expressing it freely and often, not just to God but to those around us.

Lastly, nurturing a pure heart might be the most challenging yet rewarding endeavor. Actively distancing oneself from negative influences and seeking God's guidance in every situation can lead to a heart full of gratitude and devoid of malice.

CHAPTER'S REFLECTION

- Gratitude is not just an emotional response but an expected act, the laid-down principle of God.

- The seven laws of gratitude include;

  a. The Law of Reciprocity

  b. Law of Worship

  c. The Law of Humility

  d. The Law of Reflection

  e. The Law of Contentment

  f. The Law of Sowing and Reaping

  g. The Law of Purity

Expressing Gratitude in Relationships

07

Gratitude, the acknowledgment of the goodness in one's life, is an emotion and virtue that strengthens relationships, nurtures emotional well-being, and builds a sense of community. Expressing gratitude to others is a powerful way of communicating appreciation, fostering positivity, and forging deeper connections.

Relationships, whether with partners, family, or friends, form the backbone of our lives. They provide us with support, love, companionship, and an essential sense of belonging. Expressing gratitude in relationships is essential for maintaining healthy and strong connections with others. Gratitude not only makes the other person feel appreciated and valued but also strengthens the bond between individuals. While various elements contribute to the longevity and health of a relationship, gratitude stands out as a crucial ingredient. Expressing appreciation for small and big gestures alike is a simple yet powerful tool for nurturing and solidifying the bonds we hold dear.

The Power of a "Thank You"

Gratitude has the transformative power of turning mundane moments into memories and minor gestures into monumental acts of love. The simplest and most direct way to express gratitude is by saying "thank you" sincerely and regularly. Whether it is for a favor, a kind gesture, or emotional support, these two words can go a long way in conveying your appreciation. When you show appreciation for a partner's gesture, such as cooking dinner or helping with chores, it sends a clear message: "I see you. I value your efforts. You matter to me." Offer sincere compliments and praise to acknowledge the positive qualities and actions of the other person. Let them know why you admire and value them. This recognition can invigorate the relationship, fueling the desire to continue to care for and be there for each other.

Appreciation in a relationship offers numerous benefits that contribute to its health, strength, and overall well-being. When people express themselves and feel appreciated, it creates a positive and nurturing environment. Below are some of the benefits of appreciation in relationships:

1. Fostering Deeper Connections

Feeling valued and appreciated helps people open up, leading to deeper and more meaningful conversations and interactions. Appreciation strengthens the emotional connection between people. It helps build trust and a sense of security, which are crucial for a lasting and fulfilling relationship. Gratitude encourages partners and friends to share their feelings, hopes, and fears without fear of being taken for granted. When people believe their emotions and efforts are appreciated, they are more likely to express themselves openly, fostering a deeper connection.

Gratitude, when expressed sincerely, is a bridge that connects hearts. It validates the contributions and sacrifices of others and makes them feel valued and important. This deepens trust and mutual respect.

> *"Let the peace of Christ rule in your hearts, since as members of one body you were called to peace. And be thankful."*
> *(Colossians 3:15)*

2. A Buffer Against Resentment

In relationships, it is natural for disagreements and misunderstandings to arise. Over time, if these feelings are not addressed, they can lead to resentment. In times of conflict, a history of appreciation can serve as a buffer. It reminds friends and partners of their positive deeds for each other and can facilitate more constructive conflict resolution and problem-solving. Couples and friends can navigate challenges more harmoniously by focusing on the positive and expressing appreciation. Instead of dwelling on the negatives, gratitude shifts the perspective towards recognizing the good in the other person.

3. Enhancing Overall Relationship Satisfaction

Multiple studies have shown a direct correlation between gratitude and relationship satisfaction. When individuals frequently express gratitude towards their partners or friends, they often experience heightened feelings of love, trust, and commitment. This sense of satisfaction leads to a decrease in breakups and enhances the overall quality of the relationship. When partners feel valued and cherished, they are more likely to report higher levels of overall happiness in the relationship.

4. Emotional Well-being

Gratitude has a profound and positive effect on emotional well-being. When individuals practice gratitude regularly, it increases positive emotions such as happiness, joy, and contentment. It helps individuals focus on the good things in life, which can counteract negative emotions like anxiety and depression. Gratitude can mitigate negative emotions such as envy, resentment, and regret. By shifting the focus from what is lacking to what's appreciated, individuals are less likely to dwell on negative thoughts and feelings, feeling more fulfilled and content.

"I will praise thee, O LORD, with my whole heart; I will shew forth all thy marvelous works."
(Psalm 9:1)

Beyond Romantic Relationships

The beauty of gratitude is that its impact goes beyond romantic relationships. We can strengthen family ties and friendships by incorporating gratitude into our daily lives. Parents expressing appreciation for their children's efforts, friends acknowledging each other's support, or siblings valuing each other's presence can profoundly impact the fabric of these relationships.

The magic of gratitude lies in its simplicity. A simple 'thank you' or a gesture of appreciation can be the cornerstone of strong, long-lasting relationships. As we navigate the complexities of human connections, it's essential to remember that showing gratitude isn't just a courteous act but a pillar upon which successful relationships are built.

How to Express Gratitude to Others

1. Verbal Appreciation

Verbal appreciation, though often overlooked, carries an incredible power to transform interpersonal relationships, whether they are in professional environments or intimate settings. It is the essence of recognizing and affirming someone's worth and the value of their contributions.

Human beings inherently seek validation. When we are children, we seek acknowledgment from our parents, teachers, and peers. As adults, this desire doesn't diminish; it merely evolves.

For example, employees who feel appreciated are more likely to be engaged and committed to their jobs. In relationships, couples who regularly express gratitude and appreciation for each other tend to have stronger bonds.

Several psychological theories, including Maslow's hierarchy of needs, emphasize the human need for belonging and esteem. Verbal appreciation directly taps into these needs by validating the individual's efforts and worth.

It's essential to differentiate between genuine appreciation and flattery. While the former is sincere and comes from a place of gratitude, the latter can often be superficial, with potential ulterior motives behind it. Authentic verbal appreciation is characterized by specificity and relevance. Instead of just saying, "You did a great job," it's more impactful to say, "The way you handled that situation was impressive because..."

The act of verbal appreciation can lead to a chain of positive events. Consider the example of Peter and his wife. Peter's acknowledgment of his wife's role in their shared journey wasn't just a fleeting comment; it prompted a more profound reflection on their relationship. This sort of ripple effect can manifest in various ways:

a. Increased Confidence: When someone is appreciated, their self-worth is affirmed, boosting their confidence.

b. Strengthened Bonds: Regularly expressing appreciation

in relationships can help deepen trust and understanding between parties.

c. Promotion of Open Dialogue: As seen in Peter's case, a simple acknowledgment can lead to more in-depth, meaningful conversations.

When one person starts expressing gratitude, it can encourage others to do the same, creating a more positive environment, whether at home, among friends, or in the workplace. *"Anxiety weighs down the heart, but a kind word cheers it up."* (Proverbs 12:25)

2. The Unique Charm of Handwritten Notes

In an era dominated by screens and ephemeral messages, the act of putting pen to paper seems like an almost archaic ritual. Digital communication is no doubt efficient. A text message, an email, or a social media post can reach the intended recipient in seconds, sometimes traversing thousands of miles. But what these methods gain in speed, they often lose in depth and personal touch. Enter the charm of handwritten notes.

Handwritten notes are not just words; they are emotions frozen in time. The very act of writing by hand means that more effort and thought are put into the message. Unlike typing, where corrections can be made instantly, writing requires a level of intent. The loops, the cursive, and even the occasional strikethrough tell their own story. Every little imperfection on the paper, every ink smear, and the weight of the handwriting all carry an emotional resonance that digital fonts simply cannot replicate.

When you hold a handwritten note, you essentially touch a part of the sender's world. Unlike a digital message that lives in the nebulous realm of bytes and pixels, it's a tangible connection. Whether scribbled on a Post-it, drafted on elegant stationery, or hastily jotted down on the corner of a book page, these notes have been touched by another human. There's a sense of closeness that this physicality brings.

Rachel's Keepsake: The Lasting Impact of Handwritten Notes

For educators, the teaching journey is often filled with moments of doubt. Are they making an impact? Are they genuinely influencing the young minds they interact with daily? Rachel's note became a tangible reminder of the positive impact a teacher can make. In moments of doubt, a look at that handwritten piece of paper could provide a jolt of inspiration and motivation. The message from Rachel was a testament to the Bible verse, "Let us not become weary in doing good, for at the proper time we will reap a harvest if we do not give up." (Galatians 6:9).

Such is the power of these small tokens. They're more than just notes; they're anchors that ground us to specific moments in our lives. They remind us of the feelings we had when we first received them, and often, they provide solace or motivation in times of need.

3. Gifts

The act of gifting is a universal gesture, spanning across cultures, religions, and ages. At its core, the essence of a gift is an expression of one's feelings; it's a physical manifestation of an emotion, sentiment, or memory.

In today's materialistic world, there's often an undue emphasis on the price tag. It's easy to assume that a more expensive gift may convey deeper sentiments or express greater appreciation. However, the true essence of a gift lies not in its monetary value but in the sentiment it embodies. A handmade letter can hold more emotional weight than a diamond necklace, for instance, if the letter conveys genuine feelings of love, appreciation, and care.

The Thought Behind the Gift

Consider the book "Emma" gifted. To an outsider, it might just seem like any other book, possibly picked up from a nearby bookstore. However, for the recipient, it was a treasure trove of shared experiences and passionate discussions about literature. Every page might remind them of a particular conversation, a shared laugh, or a debated interpretation. The book, therefore, becomes more than just a collection of words; it becomes a repository of memories.

This underscores a critical aspect of gifting: the thought and intent behind the gift matter immensely. A gift should resonate with the recipient, reminding them of shared experiences, jokes, passions, or simply the giver's appreciation and love.

The quote from James 1:17 delves deeper into the spiritual significance of gifts. "Every good and perfect gift is from above" suggests that every act of kindness, every expression of love, and every gesture that brings joy is divinely inspired. Whether one is religious or not, the essence of this statement is profound: genuine gifts are pure, filled with love, and an expression of something higher and more significant than mere transactional exchanges.

4. Quality Time

The concept of time is manifold. We often hear phrases like "time is money" or "time flies." Yet, in the realm of human relationships, it's the quality, not the quantity of time, that holds paramount significance. Quality time, as a form of communication, love, and investment, is the tangible way we exhibit our commitment to relationships, reinforcing them in the process.

In an age of rapid digital communication, where connections are often reduced to fleeting texts or online "likes," spending quality time with someone speaks volumes. It is an act of setting aside distractions, undividedly immersing oneself in the moment, and giving the rarest gift one can offer: genuine attention. This gift of presence tells the recipient, "You matter to me. This moment, right here and now, is ours."

Celebrating Bonds: Mark's Day Out

Consider an instance of Mark and his mother. Their day out wasn't about checking off items from a to-do list or merely filling up hours. It was about enriching their bond, reminiscing about shared memories, and dreaming of the future. This day will be etched in their memories, not for what they did but for how they felt—understood, valued, and closer than ever.

Such occasions often lead to sharing hopes, dreams, fears, and unresolved feelings. These moments of deep connection pave the way for mutual understanding and strengthened bonds.

5. Public Praise

In a world that often fixates on individual achievements, the art of public praise often goes unnoticed. However, its effects are profound. Public acknowledgment serves as a beacon of recognition, ensuring that individuals' hard work and dedication don't go unseen. Beyond just a mere "thank you," it becomes a communal celebration of one's contributions.

Recognition is a fundamental human need. It not only affirms our efforts but also strengthens our commitment to the cause. When someone publicly acknowledges another's contributions, it creates a ripple effect. The person being praised feels valued and more motivated to continue their efforts, while observers gain a deeper understanding of the significance of those efforts.

The Power of Storytelling

Take the example of Lily's acknowledgment of her mentor at a community event. This gesture did more than just express gratitude. By sharing her experience with mentorship, Lily essentially told a story, allowing others to gain insight into the transformative power of guidance and support. Such stories inspire, reminding everyone of the tangible impact individuals can have on one another's lives.

Public praise is pivotal in fostering a culture of gratitude. When people regularly witness and participate in acts of acknowledgment, it becomes second nature to recognize the efforts of others. Communities that prioritize public praise tend to be more cohesive, fostering connections between members.

The significance of encouragement and acknowledgment isn't just a modern concept. In 1 Thessalonians 5:11, the Bible emphasizes the importance of mutual encouragement and building each other up. The verse reflects the age-old wisdom of the benefits of communal support. By uplifting one another, communities can thrive with members who are more resilient, motivated, and committed to their shared goals.

It's essential to understand that the effects of public praise extend far beyond the immediate moment of acknowledgment. Those who witness such praise are more likely to engage in similar gestures, perpetuating a cycle of gratitude and recognition.

Additionally, it serves as a learning opportunity, educating community members about the importance and impact of various roles and contributions within the community.

In recognizing the efforts of others, we don't just express our gratitude; we amplify the significance of their contributions, ensuring that their impact resonates throughout the community.

CHAPTER'S REFLECTION

- Remember that expressing gratitude should be genuine and come from the heart. It is not just about saying the words but also demonstrating through your actions and behaviors that you truly value the relationship.

- Regularly practicing gratitude in your relationships with people can lead to greater trust, understanding, and overall happiness for both you and your loved ones.

- Small gestures of appreciation and heartfelt words of thanks can have a significant impact on the overall quality of your connection with someone.

Teaching Gratitude to the Next Generation

08

A life graced with gratitude is one steeped in joy, purpose, and resilience. As society evolves, the imperative need to embed gratitude in the hearts of the younger generation becomes even more pronounced. Gratitude not only promotes a healthy spiritual and emotional demeanor but also aligns with the biblical instruction to *"train up a child in the way he should go"* (Proverbs 22:6). This beckons us, as caregivers, educators, and faith leaders, to ensure gratitude is not merely taught but is deeply felt and lived by our children. Teaching gratitude to the next generation is a valuable life lesson that can help children grow into emotionally healthy and empathetic individuals. Gratitude fosters positive attitudes, enhances relationships, and promotes overall well-being.

Biblical Models of Generational Gratitude

The Bible contains numerous examples of individuals who served as icons and role models for teaching the next generation the act of gratitude. Here are a few notable biblical figures who exemplified and passed down the importance of gratitude:

Abraham and Isaac

Abraham is often referred to as the father of faith in the Bible. Abraham's journey, marked by his willingness to obey God even in difficult circumstances, demonstrated trust, unwavering faith, and profound gratitude for God's promises, setting a powerful precedent for his son, Isaac. In Genesis 22:7-8, the poignant exchange between father and son reveals Isaac's implicit trust, mirroring Abraham's deep-rooted faith. Abraham's gratitude for God's promises was evidently passed on, shaping Isaac's spiritual foundation.

"Isaac spoke up and said to his father Abraham, Father? Yes, my son? Abraham replied. The fire and wood are here, Isaac said, but where is the lamb for the burnt offering? Abraham answered, God himself will provide the lamb for the burnt offering, my son. And the two of them went on together."

Abraham's faith and gratitude were passed down to his descendants, who looked to him as a model of faithful obedience.

Timothy and his mother and grandmother

Timothy stands as a testament to the generational transfer of faith and gratitude. 2 Timothy 1:5 highlights the spiritual legacy, tracing from grandmother Lois to mother Eunice and eventually residing powerfully in Timothy. This lineage underscores the importance of intergenerational teachings of gratitude and faith.

"I am reminded of your sincere faith, which first lived in your grandmother Lois and in your mother Eunice and, I am persuaded, now lives in you also."

King David

David, known for his psalms and songs of praise, was a man of deep gratitude. He expressed his thankfulness to God through his poetry and music. The Psalms, many of which were written by David, contain numerous expressions of gratitude and praise, setting a powerful example for the coming generations.

Modern Challenges to Cultivating Gratitude in Youth

The Entitlement Culture

Today's culture often feeds a sense of entitlement, where privileges are expected, and gratitude is overlooked. This mindset poses a challenge to instilling genuine thankfulness. By turning to biblical teachings, we can emphasize the virtues of humility, contentment, and recognizing God's hand in all things, thus counteracting the entitlement culture.

Technology and Instant Gratification

The digital age, while having its merits, often fosters impatience, with everything available at the click of a button. This hinders the ability to appreciate gradual blessings and long-term growth. Technology has conditioned young people to expect immediate rewards and gratification. Gratitude, on the other hand, is a mindset that often requires patience and reflection. The desire for quick rewards can make it challenging for youth to embrace gratitude, which is a more gradual and ongoing process. Biblical wisdom, emphasizing patience, hope, and God's perfect timing, can offer a counternarrative to the rush of instant gratification. On the other hand, by fostering a mindful approach to technology and instilling the importance of gratitude, adults can help young people develop a deeper appreciation for life's blessings in our fast-paced, tech-driven world.

Materialism and Consumerism

Advertisements and marketing messages bombard young people with the idea that happiness and success are linked to material possessions. This materialistic culture can shift their focus away from appreciating intangible blessings like relationships, experiences, and personal growth.

Practical Steps for Instilling Gratitude in Children

Modeling Gratitude

Children often learn by emulation. Living a life saturated in gratitude, where thankfulness is expressed openly and frequently, serves as a potent lesson for the young ones, teaching them more effectively than mere words ever could. Just as Jesus showcased humility and thankfulness throughout his life, serving as an example for his disciples and followers, adults can be role models for the children around them. "And whatever you do, whether in word or deed, do it all in the name of the Lord Jesus, giving thanks to God the Father through him" (Colossians 3:17). This passage underscores the importance of embodying gratitude in all aspects of life, allowing children to see it as a norm rather than an exception.

By modeling gratitude, we gift our children a lens through which they can perceive the world positively and interact with it meaningfully.

Gratitude journaling and family sharing

Encouraging children to jot down daily blessings or initiating family sessions to share moments of gratitude can foster a consistent practice of thankfulness, making it an integral part of their lives.

Gratitude is more than just saying "thank you." It is a mindset, an approach to life, that emphasizes the positive and recognizes the good in every situation, even during challenges. One of the most effective ways to cultivate this perspective is through gratitude journaling and family sharing. When combined with scriptural teachings, this practice can instill values that last a lifetime.

Biblical Storytelling

As parents, educators, or mentors, it is essential to instill this virtue in the hearts of young children, enabling them to grow into appreciative and compassionate adults.

One of the most potent tools at our disposal is the art of

storytelling, and the Bible offers a rich tapestry of narratives that emphasize gratitude. Through the stories of individuals who showed or were taught gratitude, children can derive valuable lessons that will remain with them for a lifetime.

We referred to a story like that of King David in the previous chapter. Despite facing numerous challenges, he consistently expressed his gratitude towards God. Psalms like Psalm 23 ("The Lord is my shepherd, I shall not want") and Psalm 103 ("Bless the Lord, O my soul") are filled with David's heartfelt appreciation for God's blessings and mercies. David's life was not always smooth sailing. From facing giants to running for his life, David encountered numerous challenges. Yet his psalms showcase his unwavering gratitude. Children can learn that there's always something to be grateful for, regardless of life's ups and downs.

After narrating a story, relate it to situations in their daily lives. For instance, after sharing the story, ask them about a time they felt thankful and discuss the importance of expressing that gratitude.

Acts of Service

While verbal affirmations of thankfulness are valuable, there is another, perhaps even more profound, way to instill gratitude in children: by involving them in acts of service. When children actively aid others, they begin to appreciate their blessings and develop a deeper understanding of the human experience.

Often, children are sheltered from the more challenging facets of life, leading to a skewed perception of reality. Acts of service expose them to different life situations, from the challenges faced by the homeless to the struggles of children in orphanages or the difficulties faced by the elderly. These experiences help them recognize that the world is vast, diverse, and filled with a myriad of stories.

Acts of service are not just about giving; they are about connecting. When children help others, they engage in an emotional exchange that fosters empathy. They learn to see the world through another's eyes, and in doing so, they come to understand the emotions, needs, and aspirations of those they serve.

By serving others, children get a firsthand look at privilege—or the lack of it. They begin to understand that things they might take for granted, such as a warm bed, regular meals, or educational opportunities, aren't accessible to everyone. This realization can be a powerful catalyst for gratitude.

The Legacy of a Grateful Heart

Raising a generation entrenched in gratitude promises a brighter, more compassionate future. A heart filled with gratitude is spiritually attuned and more empathetic, joyful, and resilient. This monumental task isn't just the duty of parents but of the entire community—churches, schools, and societal institutions. When gratitude becomes the cornerstone of the next generation's ethos, we can anticipate a world anchored in love, faith, and true contentment. The torch of gratitude once passed on, has the power to illuminate the world, one thankful heart at a time.

Examples Worth Sharing

1. The Gratitude Project

The Gratitude Project is an organization that successfully implemented the strategy of cultivating a gratitude community. They started by organizing gratitude circles in local communities, where individuals would gather to share their gratitude and appreciation for one another. These circles provided a safe and supportive space for individuals to express gratitude, fostering connection and positivity. As the circles grew in popularity, The Gratitude Project expanded its reach by organizing larger gratitude events and workshops, inviting people from all walks of life to come together and celebrate gratitude. Through their efforts, they inspired and encouraged countless individuals to embrace a life of gratitude, creating a ripple effect of appreciation and kindness in their communities.

2. The Thank-You Notes Initiative

A corporate organization implemented the strategy of sharing gratitude with others through the Thank-You Notes Initiative. Every employee was encouraged to write personalized thank-you notes to their colleagues, expressing gratitude for their contributions and support. These notes were then placed in designated gratitude boxes, and each week, a team member would collect the notes and distribute them to the recipients. This simple yet powerful act of gratitude created a culture of appreciation within the organization, boosting morale, fostering stronger relationships, and inspiring others to adopt a grateful mindset. The Thank-You Notes Initiative enhanced employee satisfaction and improved teamwork and collaboration, increasing productivity and creating a more positive work environment.

3. The Gratitude Journal Club

A group of friends formed a Gratitude Journal Club, inspired by the strategy of encouraging gratitude journaling. They decided to meet once a week to share their journal entries and discuss their experiences with gratitude. Each member would take turns leading the group, offering prompts and guiding discussions on different aspects of gratitude. Through this club, they deepened their gratitude practice and inspired and encouraged one another to continue embracing gratitude daily. Over time, the club expanded, and more individuals joined, creating a supportive community of like-minded individuals who shared their gratitude journeys, provided encouragement, and celebrated each other's growth. The Gratitude Journal Club became a source of inspiration and motivation for its members, reinforcing the importance of gratitude and its transformative power.

CHAPTER'S REFLECTION

- Teaching gratitude is not just about instructing children but also about fostering a mindset and attitude of appreciation.

- By incorporating practical steps for fostering gratitude into your family's daily lives, you can help the next generation develop a deep sense of gratitude that will benefit them throughout their lives.

ALLOW GOD TO TRANSFORM BATTLES INTO BLESSINGS!

The word beracah means a blessing. The valley of fear, worry, pain, burden, sorrow, and battles was renamed the valley of blessings. God wants you to live in the valley of gratitude and blessings, not in the valley of battles. He wants you to live in the valley of Beracah!

God says, "I don't want you to live in the valley of ungratefulness and battles anymore; I want you to live in the valley of blessings."

The purpose of this book is to unlock the power of gratitude in you, thereby giving you wings to soar into a new dimension of a personal relationship with God and scale your life with meaning and purpose!

www.ingramcontent.com/pod-product-compliance
Lightning Source LLC
Chambersburg PA
CBHW071011120626
46546CB00003B/1039